Study Guide Solutions
Chapters 10-15

College Accounting
Twenty-first Edition

James A. Heintz, DBA, CPA
Professor of Accounting
School of Business
University of Kansas

Robert W. Parry, Jr., Ph.D.
Professor of Accounting
Kelley School of Business
Indiana University

SOUTH-WESTERN
CENGAGE Learning·

Australia · Brazil · Japan · Korea · Mexico · Singapore · Spain · United Kingdom · United States

ISBN-13: 978-1-285-05940-2
ISBN-10: 1-285-05940-9

South-Western Cengage Learning
5191 Natorp Boulevard
Mason, OH 45040
USA

Cengage Learning is a leading provider of customized learning solutions with office locations around the globe, including Singapore, the United Kingdom, Australia, Mexico, Brazil, and Japan. Locate your local office at: **international.cengage.com/region**.

Cengage Learning products are represented in Canada by Nelson Education, Ltd.

For your course and learning solutions, visit **www.cengage.com**.

Purchase any of our products at your local college store or at our preferred online store **www.CengageBrain.com**.

Printed in the United States of America
1 2 3 4 5 6 7   17 16 15 14 13

Table of Contents

CHAPTER 10

REVIEW QUESTIONS

1. merchandising
2. sale
3. sales ticket (or cash register receipt)
4. purchase order
5. sales invoice
6. sales return
7. sales allowances
8. credit memo
9. revenue
10. Accounts Receivable

11. Sales Tax Payable
12. revenue
13. cash discount
14. revenue
15. accounts receivable
16. check mark
17. accounts receivable
18. Accounts Receivable
19. schedule of accounts receivable
20. Accounts Receivable

EXERCISES

Exercise 1

Invoice
Invoice No.   *491*

Date   *July 18, 20--*
Your Order No.   *A208*

Terms   *30 days*

ROGERS BUILDING SUPPLIES, INC.
So. Adams,
Bloomington, IN 47401-3663

Sold to   *Custom Builders, Inc.*
2001 Hillside Drive
Bloomington, IN 47401-2287

Quantity	Description	Unit Price	Amount
10	*#6 Insulated steel doors*	*290.00*	*2,900.00*
15	*#28 Pine, six-panel doors*	*125.00*	*1,875.00*
			4,775.00

Exercise 2

Credit Memorandum	**ROGERS BUILDING SUPPLIES, INC.**
No. *17*	**So. Adams, Bloomington, IN 47401-3663**

Date *July 28, 20--*   To   *Custom Builders, Inc.*
2001 Hillside Drive
Bloomington, IN 47401-2287

We credit your account as follows:

Quantity	Description	Unit Price	Amount
1	*#6 Insulated steel door*	*290.00*	*290.00*

Exercise 3

GENERAL JOURNAL   PAGE

	DATE	DESCRIPTION	POST. REF.	DEBIT	CREDIT	
1		(a) Accounts Receivable/R. B. Jones		2 4 1 50		1
2		Sales			2 3 0 00	2
3		Sales Tax Payable			1 1 50	3
4		Sale No. 28				4
5						5
6		(b) Sales Returns and Allowances		3 0 00		6
7		Sales Tax Payable		1 50		7
8		Accounts Receivable/R. B. Jones			3 1 50	8
9		Returned merchandise				9
10						10
11		(c) Cash		2 1 0 00		11
12		Accounts Receivable/R. B. Jones			2 1 0 00	12
13		Received payment on account				13
14						14
15		(d) Cash		3 1 5 00		15
16		Sales			3 0 0 00	16
17		Sales Tax Payable			1 5 00	17
18		Cash sales				18
19						19
20		(e) Sales Returns and Allowances		1 5 00		20
21		Sales Tax Payable		0 75		21
22		Cash			1 5 75	22
23		Returned merchandise				23

Exercise 4

Sales		$5,010	
Less: Sales returns and allowances	$565		
Sales discounts	97	662	
Net sales		$4,348	

Exercise 5

GENERAL JOURNAL

PAGE

	DATE		DESCRIPTION	POST. REF.	DEBIT	CREDIT	
1	20-- Feb.	2	Accounts Receivable/Dresson Homes		9 8 95		1
2			Sales			9 4 24	2
3			Sales Tax Payable			4 71	3
4			Sale No. 255				4
5							5
6		12	Accounts Receivable/R. Acuff		1 0 5 00		6
7			Sales			1 0 0 00	7
8			Sales Tax Payable			5 00	8
9			Sale No. 256				9
10							10
11		23	Accounts Receivable/C. Rupert		1 1 4 83		11
12			Sales			1 0 9 36	12
13			Sales Tax Payable			5 47	13
14			Sale No. 257				14
15							15
16		24	Accounts Receivable/M. Staple		3 5 55		16
17			Sales			3 3 86	17
18			Sales Tax Payable			1 69	18
19			Sale No. 258				19
20							20
21		25	Accounts Receivable/A. Burtin		2 5 57		21
22			Sales			2 4 35	22
23			Sales Tax Payable			1 22	23
24			Sale No. 259				24
25							25

Exercise 6

GENERAL JOURNAL   PAGE

	DATE		DESCRIPTION	POST. REF.	DEBIT	CREDIT	
1	20-- Mar.	2	Cash		9 8 95		1
2			Accounts Receivable/Dresson Homes			9 8 95	2
3			Received cash on account				3
4							4
5		12	Cash		1 0 5 00		5
6			Accounts Receivable/R. Acuff			1 0 5 00	6
7			Received cash on account				7
8							8
9		15	Cash		4 2 5 00		9
10			Sales			4 0 4 76	10
11			Sales Tax Payable			2 0 24	11
12			Made cash sale				12
13							13
14		18	Cash		2 5 0 0 00		14
15			Sales			2 3 8 0 95	15
16			Sales Tax Payable			1 1 9 05	16
17			Made cash sale				17
18							18
19		23	Cash		1 1 4 83		19
20			Accounts Receivable/C. Rupert			1 1 4 83	20
21			Received cash on account				21
22							22
23		24	Cash		3 5 55		23
24			Accounts Receivable/M. Staple			3 5 55	24
25			Received cash on account				25
26							26
27		25	Cash		2 5 57		27
28			Accounts Receivable/A. Burtin			2 5 57	28
29			Received cash on account				29
30							30
31		31	Cash		22 0 0 0 00		31
32			Sales			20 9 5 2 38	32
33			Sales Tax Payable			1 0 4 7 62	33
34			Made cash sales				34

Exercise 6 (Concluded)

GENERAL JOURNAL

PAGE

	DATE		DESCRIPTION	POST. REF.	DEBIT	CREDIT	
1	20-- Mar.	31	Cash		27 4 4 0 00		1
2			Bank Credit Card Expense		5 6 0 00		2
3			Sales			26 6 6 6 67	3
4			Sales Tax Payable			1 3 3 3 33	4
5			Made credit card sales				5
6							6
7							7

PROBLEMS

Problem 7

GENERAL JOURNAL   PAGE

	DATE		DESCRIPTION	POST. REF.	DEBIT	CREDIT	
1	20-- July	1	Accounts Receivable/B. A. Smith		1 4 5 75		1
2			Sales			1 3 7 50	2
3			Sales Tax Payable			8 25	3
4			Sale No. 33				4
5							5
6		3	Sales Returns and Allowances		1 5 00		6
7			Sales Tax Payable		0 90		7
8			Accounts Receivable/B. A. Smith			1 5 90	8
9			Returned merchandise—Credit Memo #11				9
10							10
11		5	Accounts Receivable/L. L. Unis		2 3 1 08		11
12			Sales			2 1 8 00	12
13			Sales Tax Payable			1 3 08	13
14			Sale No. 34				14
15							15
16		7	Cash		3 4 4 97		16
17			Sales			3 2 5 44	17
18			Sales Tax Payable			1 9 53	18
19			Made cash sales				19
20							20
21		10	Accounts Receivable/W. P. Clark		2 2 0 48		21
22			Sales			2 0 8 00	22
23			Sales Tax Payable			1 2 48	23
24			Sale No. 35				24
25							25
26		11	Cash		1 2 9 85		26
27			Accounts Receivable/B. A. Smith			1 2 9 85	27
28			Received cash on account				28
29							29
30		13	Sales Returns and Allowances		2 2 00		30
31			Sales Tax Payable		1 32		31
32			Accounts Receivable/W. P. Clark			2 3 32	32
33			Returned merchandise—Credit Memo #12				33

Problem 7 (Concluded)

GENERAL JOURNAL

PAGE

	DATE		DESCRIPTION	POST. REF.	DEBIT	CREDIT	
1	20-- July	14	Cash		4 3 5 87		1
2			Sales			4 1 1 20	2
3			Sales Tax Payable			2 4 67	3
4			Made cash sales				4
5							5
6		16	Accounts Receivable/B. A. Smith		2 9 9 45		6
7			Sales			2 8 2 50	7
8			Sales Tax Payable			1 6 95	8
9			Sale No. 36				9
10							10
11		17	Cash		2 3 1 08		11
12			Accounts Receivable/L. L. Unis			2 3 1 08	12
13			Received cash on account				13
14							14
15		21	Cash		3 1 0 05		15
16			Sales			2 9 2 50	16
17			Sales Tax Payable			1 7 55	17
18			Made cash sales				18
19							19
20		24	Accounts Receivable/L. L. Unis		2 3 7 97		20
21			Sales			2 2 4 50	21
22			Sales Tax Payable			1 3 47	22
23			Sale No. 37				23
24							24
25		28	Cash		3 1 8 53		25
26			Sales			3 0 0 50	26
27			Sales Tax Payable			1 8 03	27
28			Made cash sales				28
29							29
30		31	Cash		1 9 7 16		30
31			Accounts Receivable/W. P. Clark			1 9 7 16	31
32			Received cash on account				32
33							33
34							34

Problem 8

1.　　　　　　　　　　　　**GENERAL JOURNAL**　　　　　　　　PAGE　7

	DATE		DESCRIPTION	POST. REF.	DEBIT	CREDIT	
1	20-- May	3	Accounts Receivable/T. A. Pigdon	122/✓	2 6 2 35		1
2			Sales	401		2 4 7 50	2
3			Sales Tax Payable	231		1 4 85	3
4			Sale No. 51				4
5							5
6		4	Accounts Receivable/J. R. Feyton	122/✓	5 8 30		6
7			Sales	401		5 5 00	7
8			Sales Tax Payable	231		3 30	8
9			Sale No. 52				9
10							10
11		6	Accounts Receivable/P. C. McMurdy	122/✓	1 0 4 94		11
12			Sales	401		9 9 00	12
13			Sales Tax Payable	231		5 94	13
14			Sale No. 53				14
15							15
16		10	Accounts Receivable/J. T. Messer	122/✓	1 8 5 50		16
17			Sales	401		1 7 5 00	17
18			Sales Tax Payable	231		1 0 50	18
19			Sale No. 54				19
20							20
21		12	Accounts Receivable/A. F. Schlitz	122/✓	3 7 6 30		21
22			Sales	401		3 5 5 00	22
23			Sales Tax Payable	231		2 1 30	23
24			Sale No. 55				24
25							25
26		13	Accounts Receivable/J. R. Feyton	122/✓	2 2 7 90		26
27			Sales	401		2 1 5 00	27
28			Sales Tax Payable	231		1 2 90	28
29			Sale No. 56				29
30							30
31		20	Accounts Receivable/P. C. McMurdy	122/✓	4 2 4 00		31
32			Sales	401		4 0 0 00	32
33			Sales Tax Payable	231		2 4 00	33
34			Sale No. 57				34

Problem 8 (Continued)

GENERAL JOURNAL

PAGE   8

	DATE		DESCRIPTION	POST. REF.	DEBIT	CREDIT	
1	20-- May	28	Accounts Receivable/J. T. Messer	122/✓	2 7 0 30		1
2			Sales	401		2 5 5 00	2
3			Sales Tax Payable	231		1 5 30	3
4			Sale No. 58				4
5							5
6							6

2.

GENERAL LEDGER

ACCOUNT   Accounts Receivable   ACCOUNT NO.   122

DATE		ITEM	POST. REF.	DEBIT	CREDIT	BALANCE DEBIT	BALANCE CREDIT
20-- May	1	Balance	✓			8 3 4 00	
	3		J7	2 6 2 35		1 0 9 6 35	
	4		J7	5 8 30		1 1 5 4 65	
	6		J7	1 0 4 94		1 2 5 9 59	
	10		J7	1 8 5 50		1 4 4 5 09	
	12		J7	3 7 6 30		1 8 2 1 39	
	13		J7	2 2 7 90		2 0 4 9 29	
	20		J7	4 2 4 00		2 4 7 3 29	
	28		J8	2 7 0 30		2 7 4 3 59	

ACCOUNT   Sales Tax Payable   ACCOUNT NO.   231

DATE		ITEM	POST. REF.	DEBIT	CREDIT	BALANCE DEBIT	BALANCE CREDIT
20-- May	3		J7		1 4 85		1 4 85
	4		J7		3 30		1 8 15
	6		J7		5 94		2 4 09
	10		J7		1 0 50		3 4 59
	12		J7		2 1 30		5 5 89
	13		J7		1 2 90		6 8 79
	20		J7		2 4 00		9 2 79
	28		J8		1 5 30		1 0 8 09

Problem 8 (Continued)

ACCOUNT Sales ACCOUNT NO. 401

DATE		ITEM	POST. REF.	DEBIT	CREDIT	BALANCE DEBIT	BALANCE CREDIT
20--							
May	3		J7		2 4 7 50		2 4 7 50
	4		J7		5 5 00		3 0 2 50
	6		J7		9 9 00		4 0 1 50
	10		J7		1 7 5 00		5 7 6 50
	12		J7		3 5 5 00		9 3 1 50
	13		J7		2 1 5 00		1 1 4 6 50
	20		J7		4 0 0 00		1 5 4 6 50
	28		J8		2 5 5 00		1 8 0 1 50

ACCOUNTS RECEIVABLE LEDGER

NAME J. R. Feyton

ADDRESS 6022 Columbia, St. Louis, MO 63139-1906

DATE		ITEM	POST. REF.	DEBIT	CREDIT	BALANCE
20--						
May	4		J7	5 8 30		5 8 30
	13		J7	2 2 7 90		2 8 6 20

NAME P. C. McMurdy

ADDRESS 1214 N. 2nd St., E. St. Louis, IL 62201-2679

DATE		ITEM	POST. REF.	DEBIT	CREDIT	BALANCE
20--						
May	1	Balance	✓			1 2 5 00
	6		J7	1 0 4 94		2 2 9 94
	20		J7	4 2 4 00		6 5 3 94

Problem 8 (Concluded)

NAME J. T. Messer

ADDRESS P.O. Box 249, Chesterfield, MO 63017-3901

DATE		ITEM	POST. REF.	DEBIT	CREDIT	BALANCE
20-- May	1	Balance	✓			1 7 7 00
	10		J7	1 8 5 50		3 6 2 50
	28		J8	2 7 0 30		6 3 2 80

NAME T. A. Pigdon

ADDRESS 1070 Purcell, University City, MO 63130-1546

DATE		ITEM	POST. REF.	DEBIT	CREDIT	BALANCE
20-- May	1	Balance	✓			2 8 0 00
	3		J7	2 6 2 35		5 4 2 35

NAME A. F. Schlitz

ADDRESS 800 Lindbergh Blvd., St. Louis, MO 63166-1546

DATE		ITEM	POST. REF.	DEBIT	CREDIT	BALANCE
20-- May	1	Balance	✓			2 5 2 00
	12		J7	3 7 6 30		6 2 8 30

3.

Leather All

Schedule of Accounts Receivable

May 31, 20--

J. R. Feyton	$	2	8 6	20
P. C. McMurdy			6 5 3	94
J. T. Messer			6 3 2	80
T. A. Pigdon			5 4 2	35
A. F. Schlitz			6 2 8	30
	$2		7 4 3	59

Problem 9

1.   **GENERAL JOURNAL**   PAGE   8

	DATE		DESCRIPTION	POST. REF.	DEBIT	CREDIT	
1	20-- June	1	Cash	101	3 0 0 00		1
2			Sales	401		2 8 5 71	2
3			Sales Tax Payable	231		1 4 29	3
4			Made cash sales				4
5							5
6		5	Cash	101	1 2 5 60		6
7			Accounts Receivable/L. Strous	122/✓		1 2 5 60	7
8			Received cash on account				8
9							9
10		10	Cash	101	2 6 3 25		10
11			Accounts Receivable/D. Manning	122/✓		2 6 3 25	11
12			Received cash on account				12
13							13
14		12	Sales Returns and Allowances	401.1	2 1 5 00		14
15			Sales Tax Payable	231	1 0 75		15
16			Accounts Receivable/Q. Striker	122/✓		2 2 5 75	16
17			Returned merchandise				17
18							18
19		18	Cash	101	5 8 25		19
20			Accounts Receivable/D. Warding	122/✓		5 8 25	20
21			Received cash on account				21
22							22
23		20	Cash	101	1 0 0 0 00		23
24			Sales	401		9 5 2 38	24
25			Sales Tax Payable	231		4 7 62	25
26			Made cash sales				26
27							27
28		21	Cash	101	2 9 99		28
29			Accounts Receivable/L. Clese	122/✓		2 9 99	29
30			Received cash on account				30
31							31
32							32
33							33
34							34

Problem 9 (Continued)

GENERAL JOURNAL
PAGE 9

	DATE		DESCRIPTION	POST. REF.	DEBIT	CREDIT	
1	20-- June	24	Sales Returns and Allowances	401.1	1 1 6 25		1
2			Sales Tax Payable	231	5 81		2
3			Accounts Receivable/R. Popielarz	122/✓		1 2 2 06	3
4			Returned merchandise				4
5							5
6		27	Cash	101	4 2 6 00		6
7			Accounts Receivable/L. LeCount	122/✓		4 2 6 00	7
8			Received cash on account				8
9							9
10		30	Cash	101	8 5 3 0 00		10
11			Bank Credit Card Expense	513	8 0 00		11
12			Sales	401		8 2 0 0 00	12
13			Sales Tax Payable	231		4 1 0 00	13
14			Credit card sales				14
15							15

2.   ## GENERAL LEDGER

ACCOUNT Cash   ACCOUNT NO. 101

DATE		ITEM	POST. REF.	DEBIT	CREDIT	BALANCE	
						DEBIT	CREDIT
20-- June	1	Balance	✓			13 2 0 0 25	
	1		J8	3 0 0 00		13 5 0 0 25	
	5		J8	1 2 5 60		13 6 2 5 85	
	10		J8	2 6 3 25		13 8 8 9 10	
	18		J8	5 8 25		13 9 4 7 35	
	20		J8	1 0 0 0 00		14 9 4 7 35	
	21		J8	2 9 99		14 9 7 7 34	
	27		J9	4 2 6 00		15 4 0 3 34	
	30		J9	8 5 3 0 00		23 9 3 3 34	

Problem 9 (Continued)

ACCOUNT   Accounts Receivable   ACCOUNT NO.   122

DATE		ITEM	POST. REF.	DEBIT	CREDIT	BALANCE DEBIT	BALANCE CREDIT
20-- June	1	Balance	✓			1 2 5 0 90	
	5		J8		1 2 5 60	1 1 2 5 30	
	10		J8		2 6 3 25	8 6 2 05	
	12		J8		2 2 5 75	6 3 6 30	
	18		J8		5 8 25	5 7 8 05	
	21		J8		2 9 99	5 4 8 06	
	24		J9		1 2 2 06	4 2 6 00	
	27		J9		4 2 6 00		

ACCOUNT   Sales Tax Payable   ACCOUNT NO.   231

DATE		ITEM	POST. REF.	DEBIT	CREDIT	BALANCE DEBIT	BALANCE CREDIT
20-- June	1	Balance	✓				1 2 5 00
	1		J8		1 4 29		1 3 9 29
	12		J8	1 0 75			1 2 8 54
	20		J8		4 7 62		1 7 6 16
	24		J9	5 81			1 7 0 35
	30		J9		4 1 0 00		5 8 0 35

ACCOUNT   Sales   ACCOUNT NO.   401

DATE		ITEM	POST. REF.	DEBIT	CREDIT	BALANCE DEBIT	BALANCE CREDIT
20-- June	1		J8		2 8 5 71		2 8 5 71
	20		J8		9 5 2 38		1 2 3 8 09
	30		J9		8 2 0 0 00		9 4 3 8 09

ACCOUNT   Sales Returns and Allowances   ACCOUNT NO.   401.1

DATE		ITEM	POST. REF.	DEBIT	CREDIT	BALANCE DEBIT	BALANCE CREDIT
20-- June	12		J8	2 1 5 00		2 1 5 00	
	24		J9	1 1 6 25		3 3 1 25	

Problem 9 (Continued)

ACCOUNT   Bank Credit Card Expense   ACCOUNT NO.   513

DATE		ITEM	POST. REF.	DEBIT	CREDIT	BALANCE DEBIT	BALANCE CREDIT
20-- June	30		J9	8 0 00		8 0 00	

ACCOUNTS RECEIVABLE LEDGER

NAME L. Clese

ADDRESS 875 Glenway Drive, Glendale, MO 63122-4112

DATE		ITEM	POST. REF.	DEBIT	CREDIT	BALANCE
20-- June	1	Balance	✓			2 9 99
	21		J8		2 9 99	

NAME L. LeCount

ADDRESS 1439 East Broad Street, Columbus, OH 43205-9892

DATE		ITEM	POST. REF.	DEBIT	CREDIT	BALANCE
20-- June	1	Balance	✓			4 2 6 00
	27		J9		4 2 6 00	

NAME D. Manning

ADDRESS 2101 Cumberland Road, Noblesville, IN 47870-2435

DATE		ITEM	POST. REF.	DEBIT	CREDIT	BALANCE
20-- June	1	Balance	✓			2 6 3 25
	10		J8		2 6 3 25	

Problem 9 (Concluded)

NAME R. Popielarz

ADDRESS 3001 Hillcrest Drive, Dallas, PA 18612-6854

DATE		ITEM	POST. REF.	DEBIT	CREDIT	BALANCE
20-- June	1	Balance	✓			1 2 2 06
	24		J9		1 2 2 06	

NAME Q. Striker

ADDRESS 4113 Main Street, Beech Grove, IN 46107-9643

DATE		ITEM	POST. REF.	DEBIT	CREDIT	BALANCE
20-- June	1	Balance	✓			2 2 5 75
	12		J8		2 2 5 75	

NAME L. Strous

ADDRESS 2215 N. State Road 135, Greenwood, IN 46142-6432

DATE		ITEM	POST. REF.	DEBIT	CREDIT	BALANCE
20-- June	1	Balance	✓			1 2 5 60
	5		J8		1 2 5 60	

NAME D. Warding

ADDRESS 1100 W. Main Street, Carmel, IN 46032-2364

DATE		ITEM	POST. REF.	DEBIT	CREDIT	BALANCE
20-- June	1	Balance	✓			5 8 25
	18		J8		5 8 25	

CHAPTER 11

REVIEW QUESTIONS

1. purchases
2. purchase requisition
3. purchase order
4. receiving report
5. purchase invoice
6. 2% cash discount
7. trade discount

8. Purchases
   Purchases Returns and
      Allowances
   Purchases Discounts
   Freight-In
9. buyer
10. seller
11. cost of merchandise sold
12. gross profit

13. accounts payable ledger
14. check mark
15. Purchases Returns and
      Allowances
16. accounts payable
17. Accounts Payable
18. schedule of accounts payable

EXERCISES

Exercise 1

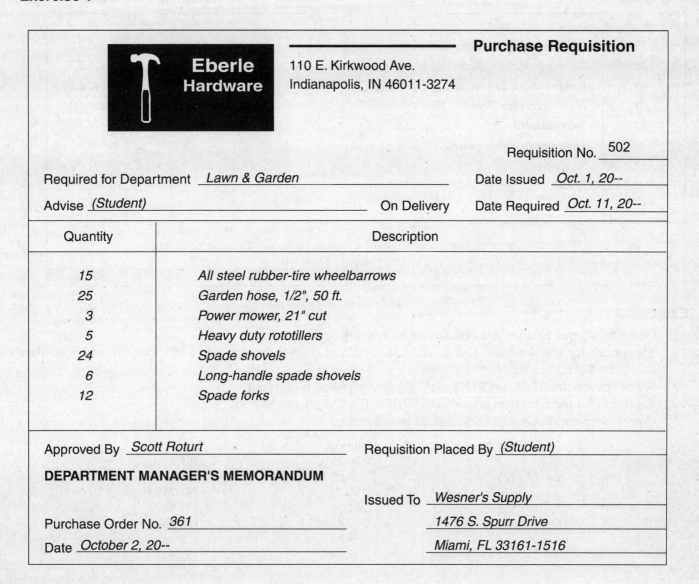

Eberle Hardware
110 E. Kirkwood Ave.
Indianapolis, IN 46011-3274

Purchase Requisition

Requisition No. _502_

Required for Department _Lawn & Garden_   Date Issued _Oct. 1, 20--_

Advise _(Student)_   On Delivery   Date Required _Oct. 11, 20--_

Quantity	Description
15	All steel rubber-tire wheelbarrows
25	Garden hose, 1/2", 50 ft.
3	Power mower, 21" cut
5	Heavy duty rototillers
24	Spade shovels
6	Long-handle spade shovels
12	Spade forks

Approved By _Scott Roturt_   Requisition Placed By _(Student)_

DEPARTMENT MANAGER'S MEMORANDUM

Issued To _Wesner's Supply_

Purchase Order No. _361_   _1476 S. Spurr Drive_

Date _October 2, 20--_   _Miami, FL 33161-1516_

Exercise 2

	Purchase Order

Eberle Hardware
110 E. Kirkwood Ave.
Indianapolis, IN 46011-3274

Order No. 361

Date _October 2, 20--_

To _Wesner's Supply_

1476 S. Spurr Drive

Miami, FL 33161-1516

Deliver By _October 11, 20--_

Ship via _AAA_

FOB _Destination_

Quantity	Description	Unit Price	Total
15	All steel rubber-tire wheelbarrows	$ 20.35	$ 305.25
25	Garden hose, 1/2", 50 ft.	4.65	116.25
3	Power mower, 21" cut	180.75	542.25
5	Heavy duty rototillers	291.50	1,457.50
24	Spade shovels	7.45	178.80
6	Long-handle spade shovels	9.30	55.80
12	Spade forks	7.70	92.40
	Total		$2,748.25

By _(Student)_

Exercise 3

1. Quantity shipped for the third item should be 3, not 4.
2. The prices for the third and fourth items are reversed. Power mowers are $180.75 each, and rototillers should be $291.50 each.
3. Spade shovels are $7.45, not $7.95 each. (*Note:* Extension is correct.)
4. Extension for the sixth item is incorrect, $9.30 × 6 = $55.80, not $57.00.
5. Correct invoice total should be $2,748.25 as follows:

Quantity	Unit Price	Total
15	$ 20.35	$ 305.25
25	4.65	116.25
3	180.75	542.25
5	291.50	1,457.50
24	7.45	178.80
6	9.30	55.80
12	7.70	92.40
		$2,748.25

Exercise 4

$800 \times 0.9 = 720

Exercise 5

1. $1,200 \times 0.97 = $1,164$ 2. $1,200 \times 0.02 = 24

Exercise 6

INCOME STATEMENT

Sales			$257,800	
Less: Sales returns and allowances		$ 1,900		
Sales discounts		400	2,300	
Net sales				$255,500
Cost of goods sold:				
Merchandise inventory, Aug. 1, 20--			$ 38,000	
Purchases		$200,000		
Less: Purchases returns & allowances	$10,200			
Purchases discounts	4,000	14,200		
Net purchases		$185,800		
Add freight-in		2,000		
Cost of goods purchased			187,800	
Goods available for sale			$225,800	
Less merchandise inv., Aug. 31, 20--			32,000	
Cost of goods sold				193,800
Gross profit				$ 61,700

Exercise 7

1. and 2.

GENERAL JOURNAL   PAGE

	DATE		DESCRIPTION	POST. REF.	DEBIT	CREDIT	
1	20-- Nov.	5	Purchases		17 2 1 5 90		1
2			Accounts Payable			17 2 1 5 90	2
3							3
4		15	Accounts Payable		17 2 1 5 90		4
5			Cash			16 8 7 1 58	5
6			Purchases Discounts			3 4 4 32	6
7							7
8	Dec.	5	Accounts Payable		17 2 1 5 90		8
9			Cash			17 2 1 5 90	9
10							10
11							11

Gross invoice:
20	@ $63.95	=	$ 1,279.00
10	@ $900.00	=	9,000.00
5	@ $1,995.00	=	9,975.00

Gross invoice	$20,254.00
Less trade discount	3,038.10
Balance	$17,215.90
Less cash discount	344.32
Net invoice price	$16,871.58

PROBLEMS
Problem 8
1.

GENERAL JOURNAL
PAGE   9

	DATE		DESCRIPTION	POST. REF.	DEBIT	CREDIT	
1	20-- Nov.	2	Purchases	501	4 1 4 5 00		1
2			Accounts Payable/Ford Distributors	202/✓		4 1 4 5 00	2
3			Invoice No. 611				3
4							4
5		5	Purchases	501	2 1 6 5 00		5
6			Accounts Payable/Mueller Wholesaler	202/✓		2 1 6 5 00	6
7			Invoice No. 216				7
8							8
9		15	Purchases	501	2 8 9 5 00		9
10			Accounts Payable/Grant White & Co.	202/✓		2 8 9 5 00	10
11			Invoice No. 399				11
12							12
13		19	Purchases	501	1 8 4 5 00		13
14			Accounts Payable/Bailey & Hinds, Inc.	202/✓		1 8 4 5 00	14
15			Invoice No. 106				15
16							16
17		22	Purchases	501	3 2 2 5 00		17
18			Accounts Payable/Ford Distributors	202/✓		3 2 2 5 00	18
19			Invoice No. 914				19
20							20
21		28	Purchases	501	2 1 7 5 00		21
22			Accounts Payable/Jackson Company	202/✓		2 1 7 5 00	22
23			Invoice No. 661				23
24							24
25		30	Purchases	501	3 5 0 0 00		25
26			Accounts Payable/Mueller Wholesaler	202/✓		3 5 0 0 00	26
27			Invoice No. 716				27
28							28
29							29
30							30

Problem 8 (Continued)

2.

GENERAL LEDGER

ACCOUNT   Accounts Payable   ACCOUNT NO.   202

DATE		ITEM	POST. REF.	DEBIT	CREDIT	BALANCE DEBIT	BALANCE CREDIT
20-- Nov.	2		J9		4 1 4 5 00		4 1 4 5 00
	5		J9		2 1 6 5 00		6 3 1 0 00
	15		J9		2 8 9 5 00		9 2 0 5 00
	19		J9		1 8 4 5 00		11 0 5 0 00
	22		J9		3 2 2 5 00		14 2 7 5 00
	28		J9		2 1 7 5 00		16 4 5 0 00
	30		J9		3 5 0 0 00		19 9 5 0 00

ACCOUNT   Purchases   ACCOUNT NO.   501

DATE		ITEM	POST. REF.	DEBIT	CREDIT	BALANCE DEBIT	BALANCE CREDIT
20-- Nov.	2		J9	4 1 4 5 00		4 1 4 5 00	
	5		J9	2 1 6 5 00		6 3 1 0 00	
	15		J9	2 8 9 5 00		9 2 0 5 00	
	19		J9	1 8 4 5 00		11 0 5 0 00	
	22		J9	3 2 2 5 00		14 2 7 5 00	
	28		J9	2 1 7 5 00		16 4 5 0 00	
	30		J9	3 5 0 0 00		19 9 5 0 00	

ACCOUNTS PAYABLE LEDGER

NAME Bailey & Hinds, Inc.

ADDRESS

DATE		ITEM	POST. REF.	DEBIT	CREDIT	BALANCE
20-- Nov.	19		J9		1 8 4 5 00	1 8 4 5 00

Problem 8 (Concluded)

NAME Ford Distributors

ADDRESS

DATE		ITEM	POST. REF.	DEBIT	CREDIT	BALANCE
20-- Nov.	2		J9		4 1 4 5 00	4 1 4 5 00
	22		J9		3 2 2 5 00	7 3 7 0 00

NAME Grant White & Co.

ADDRESS

DATE		ITEM	POST. REF.	DEBIT	CREDIT	BALANCE
20-- Nov.	15		J9		2 8 9 5 00	2 8 9 5 00

NAME Jackson Company

ADDRESS

DATE		ITEM	POST. REF.	DEBIT	CREDIT	BALANCE
20-- Nov.	28		J9		2 1 7 5 00	2 1 7 5 00

NAME Mueller Wholesaler

ADDRESS

DATE		ITEM	POST. REF.	DEBIT	CREDIT	BALANCE
20-- Nov.	5		J9		2 1 6 5 00	2 1 6 5 00
	30		J9		3 5 0 0 00	5 6 6 5 00

Problem 9

1.

GENERAL JOURNAL

PAGE 5

	DATE		DESCRIPTION	POST. REF.	DEBIT	CREDIT	
1	20-- Feb.	3	Purchases	501	4 9 8 64		1
2			Accounts Payable/Ringer's	202/✓		4 9 8 64	2
3			Invoice No. 611				3
4							4
5		4	Purchases	501	7 8 0 11		5
6			Accounts Payable/Klein Brothers	202/✓		7 8 0 11	6
7			Invoice No. 112				7
8							8
9		11	Purchases	501	2 3 0 0 00		9
10			Accounts Payable/Corleon's	202/✓		2 3 0 0 00	10
11			Invoice No. 432				11
12							12
13		15	Accounts Payable/Ringer's	202/✓	3 0 00		13
14			Purchases Returns and Allowances	501.1		3 0 00	14
15			Returned merchandise				15

Problem 9 (Continued)

2.

GENERAL LEDGER

ACCOUNT   Accounts Payable   ACCOUNT NO.   202

DATE		ITEM	POST. REF.	DEBIT	CREDIT	BALANCE DEBIT	BALANCE CREDIT
20-- Feb.	1	Balance	✓				3 1 2 5 50
	3		J5		4 9 8 64		3 6 2 4 14
	4		J5		7 8 0 11		4 4 0 4 25
	11		J5		2 3 0 0 00		6 7 0 4 25
	15		J5	3 0 00			6 6 7 4 25

ACCOUNT   Purchases   ACCOUNT NO.   501

DATE		ITEM	POST. REF.	DEBIT	CREDIT	BALANCE DEBIT	BALANCE CREDIT
20-- Feb.	1	Balance	✓			2 5 0 0 00	
	3		J5	4 9 8 64		2 9 9 8 64	
	4		J5	7 8 0 11		3 7 7 8 75	
	11		J5	2 3 0 0 00		6 0 7 8 75	

ACCOUNT   Purchases Returns and Allowances   ACCOUNT NO.   501.1

DATE		ITEM	POST. REF.	DEBIT	CREDIT	BALANCE DEBIT	BALANCE CREDIT
20-- Feb.	1	Balance	✓				2 0 0 00
	15		J5		3 0 00		2 3 0 00

Problem 9 (Concluded)

ACCOUNTS PAYABLE LEDGER

NAME Corleon's

ADDRESS 1894 Winthrop Ave., White Plains, NY 10606-6915

DATE		ITEM	POST. REF.	DEBIT	CREDIT	BALANCE
20-- Feb.	1	Balance	✓			1 6 2 5 50
	11		J5		2 3 0 0 00	3 9 2 5 50

NAME Klein Brothers

ADDRESS 1728 Camino Real, San Antonio, TX 78238-4420

DATE		ITEM	POST. REF.	DEBIT	CREDIT	BALANCE
20-- Feb.	1	Balance	✓			6 2 5 00
	4		J5		7 8 0 11	1 4 0 5 11

NAME Ringer's

ADDRESS 1500 North Street, Bakersfield, CA 93301-4747

DATE		ITEM	POST. REF.	DEBIT	CREDIT	BALANCE
20-- Feb.	1	Balance	✓			8 7 5 00
	3		J5		4 9 8 64	1 3 7 3 64
	15		J5	3 0 00		1 3 4 3 64

3.

Tom's Sporting Goods
Schedule of Accounts Payable
February 28, 20--

Corleon's	$3 9 2 5 50
Klein Brothers	1 4 0 5 11
Ringer's	1 3 4 3 64
	$6 6 7 4 25

Problem 10

1.

GENERAL JOURNAL

	DATE		DESCRIPTION	POST. REF.	DEBIT	CREDIT	
1	20-- Aug.	1	Rent Expense	521	9 0 0 00		1
2			Cash	101		9 0 0 00	2
3			Check No. 47				3
4							4
5		3	Accounts Payable/Blue Suede Shoes Company	202/✓	6 4 0 00		5
6			Cash	101		6 2 7 20	6
7			Purchases Discounts	501.2		1 2 80	7
8			Check No. 48				8
9							9
10		9	Accounts Payable/Style-Rite	202/✓	8 0 0 00		10
11			Cash	101		7 7 6 00	11
12			Purchases Discounts	501.2		2 4 00	12
13			Check No. 49				13
14							14
15		14	Utilities Expense	533	1 2 5 28		15
16			Cash	101		1 2 5 28	16
17			Check No. 50				17
18							18
19		20	Purchases	501	5 2 5 00		19
20			Cash	101		5 2 5 00	20
21			Check No. 51				21
22							22
23		22	Accounts Payable/West Coast Shoes	202/✓	6 2 5 00		23
24			Cash	101		6 2 5 00	24
25			Check No. 52				25
26							26
27		27	C. Bultman, Drawing	312	2 0 0 0 00		27
28			Cash	101		2 0 0 0 00	28
29			Check No. 53				29
30							30

Problem 10 (Continued)

2.

GENERAL LEDGER

ACCOUNT   Cash   ACCOUNT NO. 101

DATE		ITEM	POST. REF.	DEBIT	CREDIT	BALANCE	
						DEBIT	CREDIT
20-- Aug.	1	Balance	✓			25 0 0 0 00	
	1		J4		9 0 0 00	24 1 0 0 00	
	3		J4		6 2 7 20	23 4 7 2 80	
	9		J4		7 7 6 00	22 6 9 6 80	
	14		J4		1 2 5 28	22 5 7 1 52	
	20		J4		5 2 5 00	22 0 4 6 52	
	22		J4		6 2 5 00	21 4 2 1 52	
	27		J4		2 0 0 0 00	19 4 2 1 52	

ACCOUNT   Accounts Payable   ACCOUNT NO. 202

DATE		ITEM	POST. REF.	DEBIT	CREDIT	BALANCE	
						DEBIT	CREDIT
20-- Aug.	1	Balance	✓				3 3 6 6 00
	3		J4	6 4 0 00			2 7 2 6 00
	9		J4	8 0 0 00			1 9 2 6 00
	22		J4	6 2 5 00			1 3 0 1 00

ACCOUNT   C. Bultman, Drawing   ACCOUNT NO. 312

DATE		ITEM	POST. REF.	DEBIT	CREDIT	BALANCE	
						DEBIT	CREDIT
20-- Aug.	1	Balance	✓			14 0 0 0 00	
	27		J4	2 0 0 0 00		16 0 0 0 00	

ACCOUNT   Purchases   ACCOUNT NO. 501

DATE		ITEM	POST. REF.	DEBIT	CREDIT	BALANCE	
						DEBIT	CREDIT
20-- Aug.	1	Balance	✓			54 2 6 5 43	
	20		J4	5 2 5 00		54 7 9 0 43	

Problem 10 (Continued)

ACCOUNT Purchases Discounts ACCOUNT NO. 501.2

DATE		ITEM	POST. REF.	DEBIT	CREDIT	BALANCE DEBIT	BALANCE CREDIT
20-- Aug.	1	Balance	✓				3 2 5 20
	3		J4		1 2 80		3 3 8 00
	9		J4		2 4 00		3 6 2 00

ACCOUNT Rent Expense ACCOUNT NO. 521

DATE		ITEM	POST. REF.	DEBIT	CREDIT	BALANCE DEBIT	BALANCE CREDIT
20-- Aug.	1	Balance	✓			7 2 0 0 00	
	1		J4	9 0 0 00		8 1 0 0 00	

ACCOUNT Utilities Expense ACCOUNT NO. 533

DATE		ITEM	POST. REF.	DEBIT	CREDIT	BALANCE DEBIT	BALANCE CREDIT
20-- Aug.	1	Balance	✓			8 2 2 87	
	14		J4	1 2 5 28		9 4 8 15	

ACCOUNTS PAYABLE LEDGER

NAME Blue Suede Shoes Company
ADDRESS 2805 South Meridian, Indianapolis, IN 46225-3460

DATE		ITEM	POST. REF.	DEBIT	CREDIT	BALANCE
20-- Aug.	1	Balance	✓			6 4 0 00
	3		J4	6 4 0 00		

NAME Style-Rite
ADDRESS 6500 9th Street, New Orleans, LA 70115-1122

DATE		ITEM	POST. REF.	DEBIT	CREDIT	BALANCE
20-- Aug.	1	Balance	✓			1 2 0 0 00
	9		J4	8 0 0 00		4 0 0 00

Problem 10 (Concluded)

NAME West Coast Shoes

ADDRESS 705 Rialto Avenue, Fresno, CA 93705-7845

DATE		ITEM	POST. REF.	DEBIT	CREDIT	BALANCE
20-- Aug.	1	Balance	✓			1 5 2 6 00
	22		J4	6 2 5 00		9 0 1 00

3.

Bultman Shoes

Schedule of Accounts Payable

August 31, 20--

Style-Rite	$ 4 0 0 00
West Coast Shoes	9 0 1 00
	$1 3 0 1 00

Problem 11

GENERAL JOURNAL

PAGE

	DATE		DESCRIPTION	POST. REF.	DEBIT	CREDIT	
1	20-- July	5	Rent Expense		6 0 0 00		1
2			Cash			6 0 0 00	2
3			Check No. 222				3
4							4
5		12	Purchases		3 2 5 0 00		5
6			Cash			3 2 5 0 00	6
7			Check No. 223				7
8							8
9		18	Accounts Payable/Martinez Guitar Company		4 5 0 0 00		9
10			Cash			4 4 1 0 00	10
11			Purchases Discounts			9 0 00	11
12			Check No. 224				12
13							13
14		25	Notes Payable/First National Bank		2 0 0 0 00		14
15			Cash			2 0 0 0 00	15
16			Check No. 225				16
17							17
18		31	A. Demis, Drawing		5 5 0 0 00		18
19			Cash			5 5 0 0 00	19
20			Check No. 226				20

CHAPTER 11 APPENDIX

**Apx. Exercise
1.**

GENERAL JOURNAL   PAGE

	DATE		DESCRIPTION	POST. REF.	DEBIT	CREDIT	
1	20-- Apr.	2	Purchases		2 0 0 0 00		1
2			Accounts Payable			2 0 0 0 00	2
3							3
4		5	Purchases		1 8 0 0 00		4
5			Accounts Payable			1 8 0 0 00	5
6							6
7		11	Accounts Payable		2 0 0 0 00		7
8			Cash			1 9 6 0 00	8
9			Purchases Discounts			4 0 00	9
10							10
11		25	Accounts Payable		1 8 0 0 00		11
12			Cash			1 8 0 0 00	12
13							13

2.

GENERAL JOURNAL   PAGE

	DATE		DESCRIPTION	POST. REF.	DEBIT	CREDIT	
1	20-- Apr.	2	Purchases		1 9 6 0 00		1
2			Accounts Payable			1 9 6 0 00	2
3							3
4		5	Purchases		1 7 8 2 00		4
5			Accounts Payable			1 7 8 2 00	5
6							6
7		11	Accounts Payable		1 9 6 0 00		7
8			Cash			1 9 6 0 00	8
9							9
10		25	Accounts Payable		1 7 8 2 00		10
11			Purchases Discounts Lost		1 8 00		11
12			Cash			1 8 0 0 00	12
13							13

CHAPTER 12
REVIEW QUESTIONS

1. special journal
2. general journal
3. date
   sale number
   customer
   dollar amounts
4. sales
5. general
6. daily
7. Cash
8. cash receipts
9. daily
10. purchases journal
11. general journal
12. Accounts Payable Credit
13. accounts payable ledger
14. daily
15. cash payments journal
16. Cash
17. date
    check number
    account debited (if applicable)
    dollar amounts
18. daily

EXERCISES
Exercise 1

Transaction	Sales	Cash Receipts	Purchases	Cash Payments	General
a. Made payment to supplier on account.				X	
b. Sold old delivery equipment for cash.		X			
c. Sold merchandise on account.	X				
d. Purchased merchandise for cash.				X	
e. Returned merchandise to supplier for credit.					X
f. Invested additional funds in the business.		X			
g. Purchased merchandise on account.			X		

Exercise 2
1. and 2.

SALES JOURNAL PAGE

	DATE	SALE NO.	TO WHOM SOLD	POST. REF.	ACCOUNTS RECEIVABLE DEBIT	SALES CREDIT	SALES TAX PAYABLE CREDIT	
1	20-- Feb. 2	255	Dresson Homes		9 8 95	9 4 24	4 71	1
2	12	256	Ray Acuff		1 0 5 00	1 0 0 00	5 00	2
3	23	257	Clydette Rupert		1 1 4 83	1 0 9 36	5 47	3
4	24	258	Marty Staple		3 5 55	3 3 86	1 69	4
5	25	259	Angel Burtin		2 5 57	2 4 35	1 22	5
6					3 7 9 90	3 6 1 81	1 8 09	6
7								7

Exercise 3

1. and 2.

CASH RECEIPTS JOURNAL   PAGE

	DATE	ACCOUNT CREDITED	POST. REF.	GENERAL CREDIT	ACCOUNTS RECEIVABLE CREDIT	SALES CREDIT	SALES TAX PAYABLE CREDIT	CASH DEBIT	
1	20-- Mar. 2	Dresson Homes			9 8 95			9 8 95	1
2	12	Ray Acuff			1 0 5 00			1 0 5 00	2
3	15					4 0 4 76	2 0 24	4 2 5 00	3
4	18					2 3 8 0 95	1 1 9 05	2 5 0 0 00	4
5	23	Clydette Rupert			1 1 4 83			1 1 4 83	5
6	24	Marty Staple			3 5 55			3 5 55	6
7	25	Angel Burtin			2 5 57			2 5 57	7
8	31					20 9 5 2 38	1 0 4 7 62	22 0 0 0 00	8
9	31					26 6 6 6 67	1 3 3 3 33	28 0 0 0 00	9
10					3 7 9 90	50 4 0 4 76	2 5 2 0 24	53 3 0 4 90	10
11									11

Exercise 4

PURCHASES JOURNAL   PAGE

	DATE	INVOICE NO.	FROM WHOM PURCHASED	POST. REF.	PURCHASES DEBIT ACCTS. PAY. CREDIT	
1	20-- Feb. 3	611	Ringer's		4 9 8 64	1
2	4	112	Klein Brothers		7 8 0 11	2
3	11	432	Corleon's		2 3 0 0 00	3
4					3 5 7 8 75	4
5						5

GENERAL JOURNAL   PAGE

	DATE	DESCRIPTION	POST. REF.	DEBIT	CREDIT	
1	20-- Feb. 15	Accounts Payable/Ringer's		3 0 00		1
2		Purchases Returns and Allowances			3 0 00	2
3		Returned merchandise				3

Exercise 5

1. and 2.

CASH PAYMENTS JOURNAL   PAGE

	DATE	CK. NO.	ACCOUNT DEBITED	POST. REF.	GENERAL DEBIT	ACCOUNTS PAYABLE DEBIT	PURCHASES DEBIT	PURCHASES DISCOUNTS CREDIT	CASH CREDIT	
1	20-- July	5	222	Rent Expense		6 0 0 00				6 0 0 00	1
2		12	223					3 2 5 0 00		3 2 5 0 00	2
3		18	224	Martinez Guitar Company			4 5 0 0 00		9 0 00	4 4 1 0 00	3
4		25	225	Notes Payable		2 0 0 0 00				2 0 0 0 00	4
5		31	226	A. Demis, Drawing		5 5 0 0 00				5 5 0 0 00	5
6						8 1 0 0 00	4 5 0 0 00	3 2 5 0 00	9 0 00	15 7 6 0 00	6
7											7

Debit total: $ 8,100   Credit total: $ 90
                   4,500   15,760
                   3,250 $15,850
                 $15,850

PROBLEMS

Problem 6

1. and 2.

GENERAL JOURNAL   PAGE

	DATE		DESCRIPTION	POST. REF.	DEBIT	CREDIT	
1	20-- July	3	Sales Returns and Allowances		1 5 00		1
2			Sales Tax Payable		0 90		2
3			Accounts Receivable/B. A. Smith			1 5 90	3
4			Accepted returned merchandise, Credit Memo #11				4
5							5
6		13	Sales Returns and Allowances		2 2 00		6
7			Sales Tax Payable		1 32		7
8			Accounts Receivable/W. P. Clark			2 3 32	8
9			Accepted returned merchandise, Credit Memo #12				9
10							10

Problem 6 (Concluded)

SALES JOURNAL   PAGE

	DATE	SALE NO.	TO WHOM SOLD	POST. REF.	ACCOUNTS RECEIVABLE DEBIT	SALES CREDIT	SALES TAX PAYABLE CREDIT	
1	20-- July 1	33	B. A. Smith		1 4 5 75	1 3 7 50	8 25	1
2	5	34	L. L. Unis		2 3 1 08	2 1 8 00	1 3 08	2
3	10	35	W. P. Clark		2 2 0 48	2 0 8 00	1 2 48	3
4	16	36	B. A. Smith		2 9 9 45	2 8 2 50	1 6 95	4
5	24	37	L. L. Unis		2 3 7 97	2 2 4 50	1 3 47	5
6					1 1 3 4 73	1 0 7 0 50	6 4 23	6
7								7
8								8

CASH RECEIPTS JOURNAL   PAGE

	DATE	ACCOUNT CREDITED	POST. REF.	GENERAL CREDIT	ACCOUNTS RECEIVABLE CREDIT	SALES CREDIT	SALES TAX PAYABLE CREDIT	CASH DEBIT	
1	20-- July 7					3 2 5 44	1 9 53	3 4 4 97	1
2	11	B. A. Smith			1 2 9 85			1 2 9 85	2
3	14					4 1 1 20	2 4 67	4 3 5 87	3
4	17	L. L. Unis			2 3 1 08			2 3 1 08	4
5	21					2 9 2 50	1 7 55	3 1 0 05	5
6	28					3 0 0 50	1 8 03	3 1 8 53	6
7	31	W. P. Clark			1 9 7 16			1 9 7 16	7
8					5 5 8 09	1 3 2 9 64	7 9 78	1 9 6 7 51	8
9									9
10									10

Problem 7

1. and 3.

SALES JOURNAL

PAGE 1

	DATE		SALE NO.	TO WHOM SOLD	POST. REF.	ACCOUNTS RECEIVABLE DEBIT				SALES CREDIT				SALES TAX PAYABLE CREDIT				
1	20-- May	3	51	T. A. Pigdon	✓	2	6 2	35		2	4 7	50			1 4	85	1
2		4	52	J. R. Feyton	✓		5 8	30			5 5	00			3	30	2
3		6	53	P. C. McMurdy	✓	1	0 4	94			9 9	00			5	94	3
4		10	54	J. T. Messer	✓	1	8 5	50		1	7 5	00			1 0	50	4
5		12	55	A. F. Schlitz	✓	3	7 6	30		3	5 5	00			2 1	30	5
6		13	56	J. R. Feyton	✓	2	2 7	90		2	1 5	00			1 2	90	6
7		20	57	P. C. McMurdy	✓	4	2 4	00		4	0 0	00			2 4	00	7
8		28	58	J. T. Messer	✓	2	7 0	30		2	5 5	00			1 5	30	8
9						1 9	0 9	59		1 8	0 1	50		1	0 8	09	9
10						(1	2 2	)		(4	0 1	)		(2	3 1	)	10

Debit total: <u>$1,909.59</u>
Credit total: $1,801.50
            <u> 108.09</u>
            <u>$1,909.59</u>

3.

GENERAL LEDGER

ACCOUNT   **Accounts Receivable**   ACCOUNT NO.   122

DATE		ITEM	POST. REF.	DEBIT				CREDIT			BALANCE						
											DEBIT				CREDIT		
20-- May	1	Balance	✓								8	3 4	00				
	31		S1	1	9 0	9	59				2 7	4 3	59				

ACCOUNT   **Sales Tax Payable**   ACCOUNT NO.   231

DATE		ITEM	POST. REF.	DEBIT				CREDIT				BALANCE					
												DEBIT		CREDIT			
20-- May	31		S1					1	0 8	09					1	0 8	09	

ACCOUNT   **Sales**   ACCOUNT NO.   401

DATE		ITEM	POST. REF.	DEBIT				CREDIT				BALANCE					
												DEBIT		CREDIT			
20-- May	31		S1					1	8 0 1	50					1	8 0 1	50	

Problem 7 (Concluded)

2.   **ACCOUNTS RECEIVABLE LEDGER**

NAME   J. R. Feyton

ADDRESS   6022 Columbia, St. Louis, MO 63139-1906

DATE		ITEM	POST. REF.	DEBIT	CREDIT	BALANCE
20-- May	4		S1	5 8 30		5 8 30
	13		S1	2 2 7 90		2 8 6 20

NAME   P. C. McMurdy

ADDRESS   1214 N. 2nd St., E. St. Louis, IL 62201-2679

DATE		ITEM	POST. REF.	DEBIT	CREDIT	BALANCE
20-- May	1	Balance	✓			1 2 5 00
	6		S1	1 0 4 94		2 2 9 94
	20		S1	4 2 4 00		6 5 3 94

NAME   J. T. Messer

ADDRESS   P.O. Box 249, Chesterfield, MO 63017-3901

DATE		ITEM	POST. REF.	DEBIT	CREDIT	BALANCE
20-- May	1	Balance	✓			1 7 7 00
	10		S1	1 8 5 50		3 6 2 50
	28		S1	2 7 0 30		6 3 2 80

NAME   T. A. Pigdon

ADDRESS   1070 Purcell, University City, MO 63130-1546

DATE		ITEM	POST. REF.	DEBIT	CREDIT	BALANCE
20-- May	1	Balance	✓			2 8 0 00
	3		S1	2 6 2 35		5 4 2 35

NAME   A. F. Schlitz

ADDRESS   800 Lindbergh Blvd., St. Louis, MO 63166-1546

DATE		ITEM	POST. REF.	DEBIT	CREDIT	BALANCE
20-- May	1	Balance	✓			2 5 2 00
	12		S1	3 7 6 30		6 2 8 30

Problem 8

1.

GENERAL JOURNAL
PAGE 5

	DATE		DESCRIPTION	POST. REF.	DEBIT	CREDIT	
1	20-- June	12	Sales Returns and Allowances	401.1	2 1 5 00		1
2			Sales Tax Payable	231	1 0 75		2
3			Accounts Receivable/Q. Striker	122/✓		2 2 5 75	3
4			Accepted returned merchandise				4
5							5
6		24	Sales Returns and Allowances	401.1	1 1 6 25		6
7			Sales Tax Payable	231	5 81		7
8			Accounts Receivable/R. Popielarz	122/✓		1 2 2 06	8
9			Accepted returned merchandise				9
10							10

CASH RECEIPTS JOURNAL
PAGE 18

	DATE		ACCOUNT CREDITED	POST. REF.	GENERAL CREDIT	ACCOUNTS REC. CREDIT	SALES CREDIT	SALES TAX PAYABLE CREDIT	BANK CR. CARD EXP. DEBIT	CASH DEBIT	
1	20-- June	1		✓			2 8 5 71	1 4 29		3 0 0 00	1
2		5	L. Strous	✓		1 2 5 60				1 2 5 60	2
3		10	D. Manning	✓		2 6 3 25				2 6 3 25	3
4		18	D. Warding	✓		5 8 25				5 8 25	4
5		20		✓			9 5 2 38	4 7 62		1 0 0 0 00	5
6		21	L. Clese	✓		2 9 99				2 9 99	6
7		27	L. LeCount	✓		4 2 6 00				4 2 6 00	7
8		30		✓			8 2 0 0 00	4 1 0 00	8 0 00	8 5 3 0 00	8
9						9 0 3 09	9 4 3 8 09	4 7 1 91	8 0 00	10 7 3 3 09	9
10						(1 2 2)	(4 0 1)	(2 3 1)	(5 1 3)	(1 0 1)	10
11											11
12											12

Debit total: $ 80.00   Credit total: $ 903.09
            10,733.09   9,438.09
         $10,813.09   471.91
                                      $10,813.09

Problem 8 (Continued)

2. and 3.   **GENERAL LEDGER**

ACCOUNT   Cash   ACCOUNT NO. 101

DATE		ITEM	POST. REF.	DEBIT	CREDIT	BALANCE DEBIT	BALANCE CREDIT
20-- June	1	Balance	✓			13 2 0 0 25	
	30		CR18	10 7 3 3 09		23 9 3 3 34	

ACCOUNT   Accounts Receivable   ACCOUNT NO. 122

DATE		ITEM	POST. REF.	DEBIT	CREDIT	BALANCE DEBIT	BALANCE CREDIT
20-- June	1	Balance	✓			1 2 5 0 90	
	12		J5		2 2 5 75	1 0 2 5 15	
	24		J5		1 2 2 06	9 0 3 09	
	30		CR18		9 0 3 09	—	

ACCOUNT   Sales Tax Payable   ACCOUNT NO. 231

DATE		ITEM	POST. REF.	DEBIT	CREDIT	BALANCE DEBIT	BALANCE CREDIT
20-- June	1	Balance	✓				1 2 5 00
	12		J5	1 0 75			1 1 4 25
	24		J5	5 81			1 0 8 44
	30		CR18		4 7 1 91		5 8 0 35

ACCOUNT   Sales   ACCOUNT NO. 401

DATE		ITEM	POST. REF.	DEBIT	CREDIT	BALANCE DEBIT	BALANCE CREDIT
20-- June	30		CR18		9 4 3 8 09		9 4 3 8 09

ACCOUNT   Sales Returns and Allowances   ACCOUNT NO. 401.1

DATE		ITEM	POST. REF.	DEBIT	CREDIT	BALANCE DEBIT	BALANCE CREDIT
20-- June	12		J5	2 1 5 00		2 1 5 00	
	24		J5	1 1 6 25		3 3 1 25	

Problem 8 (Continued)

ACCOUNT   Bank Credit Card Expense   ACCOUNT NO.   513

DATE	ITEM	POST. REF.	DEBIT	CREDIT	BALANCE DEBIT	BALANCE CREDIT
20-- June 30		CR18	8 0 00		8 0 00	

ACCOUNTS RECEIVABLE LEDGER

NAME L. Clese

ADDRESS 875 Glenway Drive, Glendale, MO 63122-4112

DATE	ITEM	POST. REF.	DEBIT	CREDIT	BALANCE
20-- June 1	Balance	✓			2 9 99
21		CR18		2 9 99	

NAME L. LeCount

ADDRESS 1439 East Broad Street, Columbus, OH 43205-9892

DATE	ITEM	POST. REF.	DEBIT	CREDIT	BALANCE
20-- June 1	Balance	✓			4 2 6 00
27		CR18		4 2 6 00	

NAME D. Manning

ADDRESS 2101 Cumberland Road, Noblesville, IN 47870-2435

DATE	ITEM	POST. REF.	DEBIT	CREDIT	BALANCE
20-- June 1	Balance	✓			2 6 3 25
10		CR18		2 6 3 25	

Problem 8 (Concluded)

NAME R. Popielarz

ADDRESS 3001 Hillcrest Drive, Dallas, PA 18612-6854

DATE		ITEM	POST. REF.	DEBIT	CREDIT	BALANCE
20-- June	1	Balance	✓			1 2 2 06
	24		J5		1 2 2 06	

NAME Q. Striker

ADDRESS 4113 Main Street, Beech Grove, IN 46107-9643

DATE		ITEM	POST. REF.	DEBIT	CREDIT	BALANCE
20-- June	1	Balance	✓			2 2 5 75
	12		J5		2 2 5 75	

NAME L. Strous

ADDRESS 2215 N. State Road 135, Greenwood, IN 46142-6432

DATE		ITEM	POST. REF.	DEBIT	CREDIT	BALANCE
20-- June	1	Balance	✓			1 2 5 60
	5		CR18		1 2 5 60	

NAME D. Warding

ADDRESS 1100 W. Main Street, Carmel, IN 46032-2364

DATE		ITEM	POST. REF.	DEBIT	CREDIT	BALANCE
20-- June	1	Balance	✓			5 8 25
	18		CR18		5 8 25	

Problem 9

1.

PURCHASES JOURNAL   PAGE   9

	DATE		INVOICE NO.	FROM WHOM PURCHASED	POST. REF.	PURCHASES DEBIT ACCTS. PAY. CREDIT	
1	20-- Nov.	2	611	Ford Distributors	✓	4 1 4 5 00	1
2		5	216	Mueller Wholesaler	✓	2 1 6 5 00	2
3		15	399	Grant White & Co.	✓	2 8 9 5 00	3
4		19	106	Bailey & Hinds, Inc.	✓	1 8 4 5 00	4
5		22	914	Ford Distributors	✓	3 2 2 5 00	5
6		28	661	Jackson Company	✓	2 1 7 5 00	6
7		30	716	Mueller Wholesaler	✓	3 5 0 0 00	7
8						19 9 5 0 00	8
9						(501) (2 02)	9
10							10

2.

GENERAL LEDGER

ACCOUNT   Accounts Payable   ACCOUNT NO.   202

DATE	ITEM	POST. REF.	DEBIT	CREDIT	BALANCE DEBIT	BALANCE CREDIT
20-- Nov. 30		P9		19 9 5 0 00		19 9 5 0 00

ACCOUNT   Purchases   ACCOUNT NO.   501

DATE	ITEM	POST. REF.	DEBIT	CREDIT	BALANCE DEBIT	BALANCE CREDIT
20-- Nov. 30		P9	19 9 5 0 00		19 9 5 0 00	

Problem 9 (Continued)

ACCOUNTS PAYABLE LEDGER

NAME   Bailey & Hinds, Inc.

ADDRESS

DATE		ITEM	POST. REF.	DEBIT	CREDIT	BALANCE
20-- Nov.	19		P9		1 8 4 5 00	1 8 4 5 00

NAME   Ford Distributors

ADDRESS

DATE		ITEM	POST. REF.	DEBIT	CREDIT	BALANCE
20-- Nov.	2		P9		4 1 4 5 00	4 1 4 5 00
	22		P9		3 2 2 5 00	7 3 7 0 00

NAME   Grant White & Co.

ADDRESS

DATE		ITEM	POST. REF.	DEBIT	CREDIT	BALANCE
20-- Nov.	15		P9		2 8 9 5 00	2 8 9 5 00

NAME   Jackson Company

ADDRESS

DATE		ITEM	POST. REF.	DEBIT	CREDIT	BALANCE
20-- Nov.	28		P9		2 1 7 5 00	2 1 7 5 00

Problem 9 (Concluded)

NAME Mueller Wholesaler

ADDRESS

DATE		ITEM	POST. REF.	DEBIT	CREDIT	BALANCE
20-- Nov.	5		P9		2 1 6 5 00	2 1 6 5 00
	30		P9		3 5 0 0 00	5 6 6 5 00

Problem 10
1. and 2.

CASH PAYMENTS JOURNAL   PAGE 9

	DATE		CK. NO.	ACCOUNT DEBITED	POST. REF.	GENERAL DEBIT	ACCOUNTS PAYABLE DEBIT	PURCHASES DEBIT	PURCHASES DISCOUNTS CREDIT	CASH CREDIT	
1	20-- Aug.	1	47	Rent Expense	521	9 0 0 00				9 0 0 00	1
2		3	48	Blue Suede Shoes Company	✓		6 4 0 00		1 2 80	6 2 7 20	2
3		9	49	Style-Rite	✓		8 0 0 00		2 4 00	7 7 6 00	3
4		14	50	Utilities Expense	533	1 2 5 28				1 2 5 28	4
5		20	51		✓			5 2 5 00		5 2 5 00	5
6		22	52	West Coast Shoes	✓		6 2 5 00			6 2 5 00	6
7		27	53	C. Bultman, Drawing	312	2 0 0 0 00				2 0 0 0 00	7
8						3 0 2 5 28	2 0 6 5 00	5 2 5 00	3 6 80	5 5 7 8 48	8
9						(✓)	(202)	(501)	(501 .2)	(101)	9
10											10

Debit total: $3,025.28   Credit total: $ 36.80
          2,065.00   5,578.48
            525.00 $5,615.28
       $5,615.28

3.   **GENERAL LEDGER**

ACCOUNT Cash   ACCOUNT NO. 101

DATE		ITEM	POST. REF.	DEBIT	CREDIT	BALANCE DEBIT	BALANCE CREDIT
20-- Aug.	1	Balance	✓			25 0 0 0 00	
	31		CP9		5 5 7 8 48	19 4 2 1 52	

Problem 10 (Continued)

ACCOUNT   Accounts Payable   ACCOUNT NO.   202

DATE		ITEM	POST. REF.	DEBIT	CREDIT	BALANCE	
						DEBIT	CREDIT
20-- Aug.	1	Balance	✓				3 3 6 6 00
	31		CP9	2 0 6 5 00			1 3 0 1 00

ACCOUNT   C. Bultman, Drawing   ACCOUNT NO.   312

DATE		ITEM	POST. REF.	DEBIT	CREDIT	BALANCE	
						DEBIT	CREDIT
20-- Aug.	1	Balance	✓			14 0 0 0 00	
	27		CP9	2 0 0 0 00		16 0 0 0 00	

ACCOUNT   Purchases   ACCOUNT NO.   501

DATE		ITEM	POST. REF.	DEBIT	CREDIT	BALANCE	
						DEBIT	CREDIT
20-- Aug.	1	Balance	✓			54 2 6 5 43	
	31		CP9	5 2 5 00		54 7 9 0 43	

ACCOUNT   Purchases Discounts   ACCOUNT NO.   501.2

DATE		ITEM	POST. REF.	DEBIT	CREDIT	BALANCE	
						DEBIT	CREDIT
20-- Aug.	1	Balance	✓				3 2 5 20
	31		CP9		3 6 80		3 6 2 00

ACCOUNT   Rent Expense   ACCOUNT NO.   521

DATE		ITEM	POST. REF.	DEBIT	CREDIT	BALANCE	
						DEBIT	CREDIT
20-- Aug.	1	Balance	✓			7 2 0 0 00	
	1		CP9	9 0 0 00		8 1 0 0 00	

Problem 10 (Concluded)

ACCOUNT   Utilities Expense   ACCOUNT NO.   533

DATE		ITEM	POST. REF.	DEBIT	CREDIT	BALANCE DEBIT	BALANCE CREDIT
20-- Aug.	1	Balance	✓			8 2 2 87	
	14		CP9	1 2 5 28		9 4 8 15	

ACCOUNTS PAYABLE LEDGER

NAME   Blue Suede Shoes Company

ADDRESS

DATE		ITEM	POST. REF.	DEBIT	CREDIT	BALANCE
20-- Aug.	1	Balance	✓			6 4 0 00
	3		CP9	6 4 0 00		

NAME   Style-Rite

ADDRESS

DATE		ITEM	POST. REF.	DEBIT	CREDIT	BALANCE
20-- Aug.	1	Balance	✓			1 2 0 0 00
	9		CP9	8 0 0 00		4 0 0 00

NAME   West Coast Shoes

ADDRESS

DATE		ITEM	POST. REF.	DEBIT	CREDIT	BALANCE
20-- Aug.	1	Balance	✓			1 5 2 6 00
	22		CP9	6 2 5 00		9 0 1 00

CHAPTER 13

REVIEW QUESTIONS

1. understated
2. understated
3. periodic system
   perpetual system
4. perpetual
5. physical inventory
6. natural business year
7. inventory sheet

8. free on board
9. destination
10. specific identification
    weighted-average
    LIFO
    FIFO
11. FIFO
12. LIFO
13. FIFO

14. LIFO
15. replacement cost
16. gains
    losses
17. inventory
18. Loss on Write-Down of
    Inventory
19. gross profit
20. retail

EXERCISES

Exercise 1

1. Periodic Inventory System

GENERAL JOURNAL   PAGE

	DATE		DESCRIPTION	POST. REF.	DEBIT	CREDIT	
1	20-- Apr.	2	Purchases		2 5 0 0 00		1
2			Accounts Payable			2 5 0 0 00	2
3							3
4		5	Purchases		3 0 0 0 00		4
5			Cash			3 0 0 0 00	5
6							6
7		10	Accounts Receivable		5 0 0 00		7
8			Sales			5 0 0 00	8
9							9
10		15	Cash		4 0 0 00		10
11			Sales			4 0 0 00	11
12							12
13							13
14							14
15							15
16							16
17							17
18							18
19							19

Exercise 1 (Concluded)
2. Perpetual Inventory System

GENERAL JOURNAL

PAGE

	DATE		DESCRIPTION	POST. REF.	DEBIT	CREDIT	
1	20-- Apr.	2	Merchandise Inventory		2 5 0 0 00		1
2			Accounts Payable			2 5 0 0 00	2
3							3
4		5	Merchandise Inventory		3 0 0 0 00		4
5			Cash			3 0 0 0 00	5
6							6
7		10	Accounts Receivable		5 0 0 00		7
8			Sales			5 0 0 00	8
9							9
10		10	Cost of Goods Sold		3 0 0 00		10
11			Merchandise Inventory			3 0 0 00	11
12							12
13		15	Cash		4 0 0 00		13
14			Sales			4 0 0 00	14
15							15
16		15	Cost of Goods Sold		2 5 0 00		16
17			Merchandise Inventory			2 5 0 00	17
18							18
19							19
20							20
21							21
22							22
23							23
24							24
25							25
26							26
27							27
28							28
29							29
30							30
31							31
32							32
33							33

Exercise 2

Cost of goods sold and sales:

Year	Model	Cost	Selling Price
2009	Mercury Grand Marquis	$ 12,000	$ 13,450
2008	Ford Focus	12,400	13,992
2006	Ford Mustang	13,200	14,450
2005	Honda Accord	10,200	12,900
2005	Porsche 911	42,500	49,900
2007	Porsche Boxster	32,500	34,200
		$122,800	$138,892

Cost of ending inventory:

Year	Model	Cost
2008	Ford Explorer	$21,500
2005	Jeep Wrangler	11,400
2004	Honda CR-V	10,500
2006	BMW M5	39,500
1990	BMW 325i	4,200
		$87,100

Gross profit:

Sales	$138,892
Cost of goods sold	122,800
Gross profit	$ 16,092

Exercise 3

Item	Cost	Market Value	LCM
1	$ 20,000	$ 18,000	$ 18,000
2	45,000	48,000	45,000
3	18,000	16,000	16,000
4	88,000	90,000	88,000
	$171,000	$172,000	$ 167,000

a. LCM based on total inventory = $171,000
b. LCM based on each item = $167,000

Exercise 4

	Cost	Retail
Net purchases/goods available for sale	$140,000	$ 200,000
Less net sales for period		160,000
Inventory, December 31, at retail		$ 40,000
Ratio of cost to retail prices of merchandise available for sale ($140,000/$200,000)		× 70%
Inventory, December 31, at estimated cost		$ 28,000

PROBLEMS

Problem 5

FIFO Inventory Method

Date 20-1/ 20-2		Cost of Goods Sold			Cost of Ending Inventory		
		Units	Unit Price	Total	Units	Unit Price	Total
	Beg. inv.	50	$120	$ 6,000		$120	$ 0
	1st purchase	80	130	10,400		130	0
	2nd purchase	100	150	15,000		150	0
	3rd purchase	50	160	8,000	20	160	3,200
	Total	280		$39,400	20		$ 3,200
Alternative calculation given goods available for sale and CGS or EI.		COG available Less cost of EI CGS		$42,600 (3,200) $39,400	COG available Less CGS Cost of EI		$ 42,600 (39,400) $ 3,200

Gross profit, FIFO:

Net sales	$54,000
Cost of goods sold	39,400
Gross profit	$14,600

LIFO Inventory Method

Date 20-1/ 20-2		Cost of Goods Sold			Cost of Ending Inventory		
		Units	Unit Price	Total	Units	Unit Price	Total
	Beg. inv.	30	$120	$ 3,600	20	$120	$ 2,400
	1st purchase	80	130	10,400		130	0
	2nd purchase	100	150	15,000		150	0
	3rd purchase	70	160	11,200		160	0
	Total	280		$40,200	20		$ 2,400
Alternative calculation given goods available for sale and CGS or EI.		COG available Less cost of EI CGS		$42,600 (2,400) $40,200	COG available Less CGS Cost of EI		$ 42,600 (40,200) $ 2,400

Gross profit, LIFO:

Net sales	$54,000
Cost of goods sold	40,200
Gross profit	$13,800

Problem 5 (Concluded)

Weighted-Average Method

Cost of Goods Available for Sale ÷ Units Available for Sale   = $42,600/300

= $142 weighted-average cost per unit

Cost of goods sold = 280 units @ $142 = $39,760
Ending inventory = 20 units @ $142 = $2,840

Gross profit, weighted-average:

Net sales	$54,000
Cost of goods sold	39,760
Gross profit	$14,240

Problem 6

Estimated inventory at May 27:

Inventory, January 1	$120,000	
Net purchases, January 1–May 27	140,000	
Cost of goods available for sale		$260,000
Estimated cost of goods sold:		
Net sales	$230,000	
Normal gross profit ($230,000 × 30%)	69,000	
Estimated cost of goods sold		161,000
Estimated inventory at May 27		$ 99,000

Problem 7

	Cost	Retail
Inventory, June 1	$200,000	$ 300,000
Net purchases, June	400,000	700,000
Merchandise available for sale	$600,000	$1,000,000
Less net sales for June		780,000
Inventory, June 30, at retail		$ 220,000
Ratio of cost-to-retail prices of merchandise available for sale ($600,000/$1,000,000)		× 60%
Estimated inventory, at cost, June 30		$ 132,000

CHAPTER 13 APPENDIX

APPENDIX EXERCISES

Apx. Exercise 1

Date	Purchases Units	Cost/ Unit	Total	Cost of Goods Sold Units	Cost/ Unit	CGS	Cum. CGS	Layer	Inventory on Hand Units	Cost/ Unit	Layer Cost	Total
9/1 (BI)								(1)	100	$6.00	$ 600	
								(2)	100	6.20	620	
								(3)	200	6.30	1,260	$2,480
9/10				200	$6.30	$1,260		(1)	100	$6.00	$ 600	
				50	6.20	310	$1,570	(2)	50	6.20	310	$ 910
9/15	600	$6.50	$3,900					(1)	100	$6.00	$ 600	
								(2)	50	6.20	310	
								(4)	600	6.50	3,900	$4,810
9/30				300	$6.50	$1,950		(1)	100	$6.00	$ 600	
								(2)	50	6.20	310	
							$3,520	(4)	300	6.50	1,950	$2,860
Cost of Goods Sold during September							$3,520*					

BI: Beginning Inventory

* $1,570
   1,950
 $3,520

Apx. Exercise 2

Date	Purchases Units	Cost/ Unit	Total	Cost of Goods Sold Units	Cost/ Unit	CGS	Cum. CGS	Cost of Purchase or (Sale)	Inventory on Hand and Average Cost per Unit Cost of Inventory on Hand	Units on Hand	Average Cost/ Unit
9/1 (BI)									$2,480	400	$6.2000
9/10				250	$6.20	$1,550	$1,550	$(1,550)	930	150	6.2000
9/15	600	$6.50	$3,900					3,900	4,830	750	6.4400
9/30				300	6.44	1,932	3,482	(1,932)	2,898	450	6.4400
Cost of Goods Sold during September							$3,482				

BI: Beginning Inventory

Apx. Exercise 3

Date	Purchases Units	Cost/ Unit	Total	Cost of Goods Sold Units	Cost/ Unit	CGS	Cum. CGS	Inventory on Hand Layer	Units	Cost/ Unit	Layer Cost	Total
10/1(BI)								(1)	100	$3.00	$ 300	
								(2)	150	3.20	480	
								(3)	250	3.50	875	$1,655
10/8				250	$3.50	$875		(1)	50	$3.00	$ 150	$ 150
				150	3.20	480						
				50	3.00	150	$1,505					
10/20	300	$3.80	$1,140					(1)	50	$3.00	$ 150	
								(4)	300	3.80	1,140	$1,290
10/31				200	$3.80	$760		(1)	50	$3.00	$ 150	
							$2,265	(4)	100	3.80	380	$ 530
Cost of Goods Sold during October							$2,265					

BI: Beginning Inventory

Apx. Exercise 4

Date	Purchases Units	Purchases Cost/ Unit	Purchases Total	COGS Units	COGS Cost/ Unit	COGS CGS	COGS Cum. CGS	Cost of Purchase or (Sale)	Cost of Inventory on Hand	Units on Hand	Average Cost/ Unit
10/1 (BI)									$1,655.00	500	$3.3100
10/8				450	$3.31	$1,489.50	$1,489.50	$(1,489.50)	165.50	50	3.3100
10/20	300	$3.80	$1,140					1,140	1,305.50	350	3.7300
10/31				200	3.73	746.00	2,235.50	(746)	559.50	150	3.7300
Cost of Goods Sold during October							$2,235.50				

BI: Beginning Inventory

APPENDIX PROBLEMS

Apx. Problem 5

Date	Purchases Units	Purchases Cost/ Unit	Purchases Total	COGS Units	COGS Cost/ Unit	COGS CGS	COGS Cum. CGS	Layer	Units	Cost/ Unit	Layer Cost	Total
2/1 (BI)								(1)	30	$6.70	$ 201	
								(2)	70	6.90	483	$ 684
2/3	400	$7.10	$2,840					(1)	30	$6.70	$ 201	
								(2)	70	6.90	483	
								(3)	400	7.10	2,840	$3,524
2/5				250	$7.10	$1,775		(1)	30	$6.70	$ 201	
								(2)	70	6.90	483	
							$1,775	(3)	150	7.10	1,065	$1,749
2/11	700	$7.20	$5,040					(1)	30	$6.70	$ 201	
								(2)	70	6.90	483	
								(3)	150	7.10	1,065	
								(4)	700	7.20	5,040	$6,789
2/13				500	$7.20	$3,600		(1)	30	$6.70	$ 201	
								(2)	70	6.90	483	
								(3)	150	7.10	1,065	
							$5,375	(4)	200	7.20	1,440	$3,189

BI: Beginning Inventory

Apx. Problem 5 (Concluded)

Date	Purchases Units	Cost/Unit	Total	Cost of Goods Sold Units	Cost/Unit	CGS	Cum. CGS	Inventory on Hand Layer	Units	Cost/Unit	Layer Cost	Total
2/16	300	$7.50	$2,250					(1)	30	$6.70	$ 201	
								(2)	70	6.90	483	
								(3)	150	7.10	1,065	
								(4)	200	7.20	1,440	
								(5)	300	7.50	2,250	$5,439
2/18	500	$7.70	$3,850					(1)	30	$6.70	$ 201	
								(2)	70	6.90	483	
								(3)	150	7.10	1,065	
								(4)	200	7.20	1,440	
								(5)	300	7.50	2,250	
								(6)	500	7.70	3,850	$9,289
2/24				500	$7.70	$3,850		(1)	30	$6.70	$ 201	
				100	7.50	750		(2)	70	6.90	483	
								(3)	150	7.10	1,065	
								(4)	200	7.20	1,440	
							$ 9,975	(5)	200	7.50	1,500	$4,689
2/25				50	$7.50	$ 375		(1)	30	$6.70	$ 201	
								(2)	70	6.90	483	
								(3)	150	7.10	1,065	
								(4)	200	7.20	1,440	
							$10,350	(5)	150	7.50	1,125	$4,314
2/28	300	$8.00	$2,400					(1)	30	$6.70	$ 201	
								(2)	70	6.90	483	
								(3)	150	7.10	1,065	
								(4)	200	7.20	1,440	
								(5)	150	7.50	1,125	
								(7)	300	8.00	2,400	$6,714
Cost of Goods Sold during February							$10,350					

Apx. Problem 6

Date	Purchases Units	Purchases Cost/Unit	Purchases Total	CGS Units	CGS Cost/Unit	CGS	Cum. CGS	Cost of Purchase or (Sale)	Cost of Inventory on Hand	Units on Hand	Average Cost/Unit
2/1 (BI)									$ 684.00	100	$6.8400
2/3	400	$7.10	$2,840					$2,840.00	3,524.00	500	7.0480
2/5				250	$7.0480	$1,762.00	$ 1,762.00	(1,762.00)	1,762.00	250	7.0480
2/11	700	7.20	5,040					5,040.00	6,802.00	950	7.1600
2/13				500	7.1600	3,580.00	5,342.00	(3,580.00)	3,222.00	450	7.1600
2/16	300	7.50	2,250					2,250.00	5,472.00	750	7.2960
2/18	500	7.70	3,850					3,850.00	9,322.00	1,250	7.4576
2/24				600	7.4576	4,474.56	9,816.56	(4,474.56)	4,847.44	650	7.4576
2/25				50	7.4576	372.88	10,189.44	(372.88)	4,474.56	600	7.4576
2/28	300	8.00	2,400					2,400.00	6,874.56	900	7.6384

Cost of Goods Sold during February $10,189.44

BI: Beginning Inventory

Apx. Problem 7

Date	Purchases Units	Cost/ Unit	Total	COGS Units	Cost/ Unit	CGS	Cum. CGS	Layer	Inventory Units	Cost/ Unit	Layer Cost	Total
7/1 (BI)								(1)	50	$5.90	$ 295	
								(2)	50	6.10	305	$ 600
7/5	400	$6.20	$2,480					(1)	50	$5.90	$ 295	
								(2)	50	6.10	305	
								(3)	400	6.20	2,480	$3,080
7/7				300	$6.20	$1,860		(1)	50	$5.90	$ 295	
								(2)	50	6.10	305	
							$1,860	(3)	100	6.20	620	$1,220
7/12	300	$6.40	$1,920					(1)	50	$5.90	$ 295	
								(2)	50	6.10	305	
								(3)	100	6.20	620	
								(4)	300	6.40	1,920	$3,140
7/15				200	$6.40	$1,280		(1)	50	$5.90	$ 295	
								(2)	50	6.10	305	
								(3)	100	6.20	620	
							$3,140	(4)	100	6.40	640	$1,860
7/18	100	$6.50	$ 650					(1)	50	$5.90	$ 295	
								(2)	50	6.10	305	
								(3)	100	6.20	620	
								(4)	100	6.40	640	
								(5)	100	6.50	650	$2,510
7/20	600	$6.80	$4,080					(1)	50	$5.90	$ 295	
								(2)	50	6.10	305	
								(3)	100	6.20	620	
								(4)	100	6.40	640	
								(5)	100	6.50	650	
								(6)	600	6.80	4,080	$6,590

Apx. Problem 7 (Concluded)

Date	Purchases Units	Cost/ Unit	Total	Cost of Goods Sold Units	Cost/ Unit	CGS	Cum. CGS	Inventory on Hand Layer	Units	Cost/ Unit	Layer Cost	Total
7/24				600	$6.80	$4,080		(1)	50	$5.90	$ 295	
				100	6.50	650		(2)	50	6.10	305	
				100	6.40	640	$8,510	(3)	100	6.20	620	$1,220
7/27				100	$6.20	$ 620		(1)	50	$5.90	$ 295	
							$9,130	(2)	50	6.10	305	$ 600
7/31	100	$6.90	$ 690					(1)	50	$5.90	$ 295	
								(2)	50	6.10	305	
								(7)	100	6.90	690	$1,290
Cost of Goods Sold during July							$9,130					

BI: Beginning Inventory

Apx. Problem 8

Date	Purchases			Cost of Goods Sold				Inventory on Hand and Average Cost Per Unit			
	Units	Cost/Unit	Total	Units	Cost/Unit	CGS	Cum. CGS	Cost of Purchase or (Sale)	Cost of Inventory on Hand	Units on Hand	Average Cost/Unit
7/1 (BI)									$ 600.00	100	$6.0000
7/5	400	$6.20	$2,480					$ 2,480.00	3,080.00	500	6.1600
7/7				300	$6.1600	$1,848.00	$1,848.00	(1,848.00)	1,232.00	200	6.1600
7/12	300	6.40	1,920					1,920.00	3,152.00	500	6.3040
7/15				200	6.3040	1,260.80	3,108.80	(1,260.80)	1,891.20	300	6.3040
7/18	100	6.50	650					650.00	2,541.20	400	6.3530
7/20	600	6.80	4,080					4,080.00	6,621.20	1,000	6.6212
7/24				800	6.6212	5,296.96	8,405.76	(5,296.96)	1,324.24	200	6.6212
7/27				100	6.6212	662.12	9,067.88	(662.12)	662.12	100	6.6212
7/31	100	6.90	690					690.00	1,352.12	200	6.7606
Cost of Goods Sold during July							$9,067.88				

BI: Beginning Inventory

CHAPTER 14

REVIEW QUESTIONS

1. work sheet
2. physical count or physical inventory
3. credit income summary
4. income summary
5. net purchases
6. goods (or merchandise) available for sale
7. cost of goods sold
8. Adjusted Trial Balance Income Statement
9. purchases
10. unearned revenue
11. current liability
12. revenue
13. contra-cost or contra-purchases
14. trial balance
15. Income Statement Balance Sheet
16. income
17. work sheet
18. Merchandise Inventory
19. Cost of Goods Sold and Cash or Accounts Receivable

EXERCISES

Exercise 1

GENERAL JOURNAL   PAGE

	DATE		DESCRIPTION	POST. REF.	DEBIT	CREDIT	
1			Adjusting Entries				1
2	20-- Dec.	31	Income Summary		60 3 0 0 00		2
3			Merchandise Inventory			60 3 0 0 00	3
4							4
5		31	Merchandise Inventory		54 8 0 0 00		5
6			Income Summary			54 8 0 0 00	6
7							7

Exercise 2

Cost of goods sold:				
Merchandise inventory, beginning			$ 33,000	
Purchases		$86,000		
Less: Purchases ret. and allow.	$4,500			
Purchases discounts	2,500	7,000		
Net purchases		$79,000		
Add freight-in		1,000		
Cost of goods purchased			80,000	
Goods available for sale			$113,000	
Less merchandise inventory, ending			41,000	
Cost of goods sold				$72,000

Exercise 3

GENERAL JOURNAL   PAGE

	DATE		DESCRIPTION	POST. REF.	DEBIT	CREDIT	
1	20-- Feb.	22	Cash		50 0 0 0 00		1
2			Unearned Ticket Revenue			50 0 0 0 00	2
3							3
4			Adjusting Entry				4
5	Dec.	31	Unearned Ticket Revenue		45 0 0 0 00		5
6			Ticket Revenue			45 0 0 0 00	6
7							7

Exercise 4

GENERAL JOURNAL   PAGE

	DATE		DESCRIPTION	POST. REF.	DEBIT	CREDIT	
1			Adjusting Entries				1
2	20-- Dec.	31	Income Summary		60 0 0 0 00		2
3			Merchandise Inventory			60 0 0 0 00	3
4							4
5		31	Merchandise Inventory		57 0 0 0 00		5
6			Income Summary			57 0 0 0 00	6
7							7
8		31	Unearned Repair Revenue		5 0 0 0 00		8
9			Repair Revenue			5 0 0 0 00	9
10							10
11		31	Supplies Expense		3 2 0 0 00		11
12			Supplies			3 2 0 0 00	12
13							13
14		31	Depreciation Expense—Building		8 0 0 0 00		14
15			Accumulated Depreciation—Building			8 0 0 0 00	15
16							16
17		31	Wages Expense		2 4 0 0 00		17
18			Wages Payable			2 4 0 0 00	18
19							19
20							20

Exercise 5

GENERAL JOURNAL

PAGE

	DATE		DESCRIPTION	POST. REF.	DEBIT	CREDIT	
1	20-- Aug.	1	Merchandise Inventory		10 0 0 0 00		1
2			Accounts Payable/Gul Paper	.		10 0 0 0 00	2
3							3
4		5	Merchandise Inventory		5 0 0 0 00		4
5			Cash			5 0 0 0 00	5
6							6
7		10	Accounts Receivable/Padam Medical Services		2 0 0 0 00		7
8			Sales			2 0 0 0 00	8
9							9
10		10	Cost of Goods Sold		1 5 0 0 00		10
11			Merchandise Inventory			1 5 0 0 00	11
12							12
13							13

Exercise 6

GENERAL JOURNAL

PAGE

	DATE		DESCRIPTION	POST. REF.	DEBIT	CREDIT	
1	20-- Dec.	31	Inventory Short and Over		2 0 0 00		1
2			Merchandise Inventory			2 0 0 00	2
3							3
4							4
5							5
6							6
7							7
8							8

PROBLEMS

Problem 7
1. and 2.

Ocean Beach Sail Shop
Work Sheet
For Year Ended December 31, 20—

Account Title	Trial Balance Debit	Trial Balance Credit	Adjustments Debit	Adjustments Credit	Adjusted Trial Balance Debit	Adjusted Trial Balance Credit	Income Statement Debit	Income Statement Credit	Balance Sheet Debit	Balance Sheet Credit	
1 Cash	27,000 00				27,000 00				27,000 00		1
2 Accounts Receivable	9,000 00				9,000 00				9,000 00		2
3 Merchandise Inventory	31,000 00		(b) 36,000 00	(a) 31,000 00	36,000 00				36,000 00		3
4 Supplies	7,500 00			(c) 5,150 00	2,350 00				2,350 00		4
5 Prepaid Insurance	4,900 00			(d) 3,025 00	1,875 00				1,875 00		5
6 Land	40,000 00				40,000 00				40,000 00		6
7 Building	60,000 00				60,000 00				60,000 00		7
8 Accum. Depr.—Building		25,000 00		(e) 7,000 00		32,000 00				32,000 00	8
9 Store Equipment	29,000 00				29,000 00				29,000 00		9
10 Accum. Depr.—Store Equipment		9,000 00		(f) 2,800 00		11,800 00				11,800 00	10
11 Accounts Payable		7,600 00				7,600 00				7,600 00	11
12 Wages Payable				(h) 1,100 00		1,100 00				1,100 00	12
13 Sales Tax Payable		6,100 00				6,100 00				6,100 00	13
14 Unearned Tour Revenue		6,800 00	(g) 4,100 00			2,700 00				2,700 00	14
15 Mortgage Payable		43,000 00				43,000 00				43,000 00	15
16 N. Smith, Capital		124,590 00				124,590 00				124,590 00	16
17 N. Smith, Drawing	33,000 00				33,000 00				33,000 00		17
18 Income Summary			(a) 31,000 00	(b) 36,000 00	31,000 00	36,000 00	31,000 00	36,000 00			18
19 Sales		122,000 00				122,000 00		122,000 00			19
20 Sales Returns and Allowances	4,200 00				4,200 00		4,200 00				20
21 Tour Revenue				(g) 4,100 00		4,100 00		4,100 00			21
22 Purchases	38,000 00				38,000 00		38,000 00				22
23 Purchases Returns and Allowances		2,600 00				2,600 00		2,600 00			23
24 Purchases Discounts		1,400 00				1,400 00		1,400 00			24
25 Freight-In	2,500 00				2,500 00		2,500 00				25
26 Wages Expense	47,000 00		(h) 1,100 00		48,100 00		48,100 00				26
27 Advertising Expense	4,800 00				4,800 00		4,800 00				27
28 Supplies Expense			(c) 5,150 00		5,150 00		5,150 00				28
29 Telephone Expense	1,800 00				1,800 00		1,800 00				29
30 Utilities Expense	7,600 00				7,600 00		7,600 00				30
31 Insurance Expense			(d) 3,025 00		3,025 00		3,025 00				31
32 Depr. Expense—Building			(e) 7,000 00		7,000 00		7,000 00				32
33 Depr. Expense—Store Equipment			(f) 2,800 00		2,800 00		2,800 00				33
34 Miscellaneous Expense	790 00				790 00		790 00				34
35	348,090 00	348,090 00	90,175 00	90,175 00	394,990 00	394,990 00	156,765 00	166,100 00	238,225 00	228,890 00	35
36 Net Income							9,335 00			9,335 00	36
37							166,100 00	166,100 00	238,225 00	238,225 00	37
38											38

Problem 8

GENERAL JOURNAL

	DATE		DESCRIPTION	POST. REF.	DEBIT	CREDIT	
1			Adjusting Entries				1
2	20-- Dec.	31	Income Summary		31 0 0 0 00		2
3			Merchandise Inventory			31 0 0 0 00	3
4							4
5		31	Merchandise Inventory		36 0 0 0 00		5
6			Income Summary			36 0 0 0 00	6
7							7
8		31	Supplies Expense		5 1 5 0 00		8
9			Supplies			5 1 5 0 00	9
10							10
11		31	Insurance Expense		3 0 2 5 00		11
12			Prepaid Insurance			3 0 2 5 00	12
13							13
14		31	Depreciation Expense—Building		7 0 0 0 00		14
15			Accumulated Depreciation—Building			7 0 0 0 00	15
16							16
17		31	Depreciation Expense—Store Equipment		2 8 0 0 00		17
18			Accumulated Depreciation—Store Equipment			2 8 0 0 00	18
19							19
20		31	Unearned Tour Revenue		4 1 0 0 00		20
21			Tour Revenue			4 1 0 0 00	21
22							22
23		31	Wages Expense		1 1 0 0 00		23
24			Wages Payable			1 1 0 0 00	24
25							25
26							26
27							27
28							28
29							29
30							30

CHAPTER 14 APPENDIX

Apx. Exercise 1

GENERAL JOURNAL   PAGE

	DATE		DESCRIPTION	POST. REF.	DEBIT	CREDIT	
1			Adjusting Entry				1
2	20-- Dec.	31	Prepaid Insurance		1 8 0 0 00		2
3			Insurance Expense			1 8 0 0 00	3
4							4
5							5

Apx. Exercise 2

GENERAL JOURNAL   PAGE

	DATE		DESCRIPTION	POST. REF.	DEBIT	CREDIT	
1	20-- Aug.	21	Supplies Expense		6 0 0 0 00		1
2			Cash			6 0 0 0 00	2
3			Purchased supplies				3
4							4
5			Adjusting Entry				5
6	Dec.	31	Supplies		1 0 0 0 00		6
7			Supplies Expense			1 0 0 0 00	7
8							8
9							9
10							10

CHAPTER 15

REVIEW QUESTIONS

1. work sheet
2. single-step
3. net sales
4. Gross profit
5. income from operations
6. net income or net loss
7. increase
   decrease
8. classified
9. liquidity
10. undepreciated cost
11. Current liabilities
12. mortgage payable
13. working capital
14. current
15. Quick
16. return on owner's equity
17. accounts receivable
    turnover
18. inventory turnover
19. temporary
20. post-closing trial balance
21. adjusting
22. zero

EXERCISES

Exercise 1

Morse Motor Company

Income Statement

For Year Ended December 31, 20-1

Revenue from sales:				
Sales			$118,300	
Less: Sales returns and allowances		$ 1,000		
Sales discounts		280	1,280	
Net sales				$117,020
Cost of goods sold:				
Merchandise inventory, Jan. 1, 20-1			$ 28,900	
Purchases		$68,000		
Less: Purchases returns and allow.	$2,140			
Purchases discounts	1,360	3,500		
Net purchases		$64,500		
Add freight-in		540		
Cost of goods purchased			65,040	
Goods available for sale			$ 93,940	
Less merchandise inv., Dec. 31, 20-1			29,600	
Cost of goods sold				64,340
Gross profit				$ 52,680
Operating expenses:				
Wages expense			$ 23,200	
Rent expense			8,000	
Supplies expense			900	
Telephone expense			2,600	
Utilities expense			3,800	
Insurance expense			1,000	
Depreciation expense—equipment			2,000	
Miscellaneous expense			300	
Total operating expenses				41,800
Income from operations				$ 10,880
Other revenues:				
Interest revenue			$ 1,900	
Other expenses:				
Interest expense			700	1,200
Net income				$ 12,080

Exercise 2

Morse Motor Company

Statement of Owner's Equity

For Year Ended December 31, 20-1

K. T. Morse, capital, January 1, 20-1		$66,740
Add additional investment		10,000
Total investment		$76,740
Net income for the year	$12,080	
Less withdrawals for the year	8,000	
Increase in capital		4,080
K. T. Morse, capital, December 31, 20-1		$80,820

Exercise 2 (Concluded)

Morse Motor Company
Balance Sheet
December 31, 20-1

Assets			
Current assets:			
Cash		$19,200	
Accounts receivable		28,500	
Merchandise inventory		29,600	
Supplies		1,800	
Prepaid insurance		1,100	
Total current assets			$ 80,200
Property, plant, and equipment:			
Equipment		$32,000	
Less accumulated depreciation—equipment		4,000	28,000
Total assets			$108,200
Liabilities			
Current liabilities:			
Accounts payable	$18,620		
Wages payable	280		
Sales tax payable	480		
Mortgage payable (current portion)	1,200		
Total current liabilities		$20,580	
Long-term liabilities:			
Mortgage payable	$ 8,000		
Less current portion	1,200	6,800	
Total liabilities			$ 27,380
Owner's Equity			
K. T. Morse, capital			80,820
Total liabilities and owner's equity			$108,200

Exercise 3

1. | Current Assets | $80,200 |
   |---|---|
   | – Current Liabilities | –20,580 |
   | | $59,620 |

2. $$\frac{\text{Current Assets}}{\text{Current Liabilities}} = \frac{\$80,200}{\$20,580} = 3.90 \text{ to } 1$$

3. $$\frac{\text{Quick Assets}}{\text{Current Liabilities}} = \frac{\$47,700}{\$20,580} = 2.32 \text{ to } 1$$

4. $$\frac{\text{Net Income}}{\text{Average Owner's Equity}} = \frac{\$12,080}{(\$66,740 + \$80,820)/2} = \frac{\$12,080}{\$73,780} = 16.4\%$$

5. $$\frac{\text{Net Credit Sales}}{\text{Average Accounts Receivable}} = \frac{\$88,000}{(\$24,200 + \$28,500)/2} = \frac{\$88,000}{\$26,350} = 3.34; 365 \div 3.34 = 109.3 \text{ days}$$

6. $$\frac{\text{Cost of Goods Sold}}{\text{Average Inventory}} = \frac{\$64,340}{(\$28,900 + \$29,600)/2} = \frac{\$64,340}{\$29,250} = 2.2; 365 \div 2.2 = 165.9 \text{ days}$$

Exercise 4

GENERAL JOURNAL

PAGE

	DATE		DESCRIPTION	POST. REF.	DEBIT	CREDIT	
1			Closing Entries				1
2	20-1 Dec.	31	Sales		118 3 0 0 00		2
3			Interest Revenue		1 9 0 0 00		3
4			Purchases Returns and Allowances		2 1 4 0 00		4
5			Purchases Discounts		1 3 6 0 00		5
6			Income Summary			123 7 0 0 00	6
7							7
8		31	Income Summary		112 3 2 0 00		8
9			Sales Returns and Allowances			1 0 0 0 00	9
			Sales Discounts			2 8 0 00	
10			Purchases			68 0 0 0 00	10
11			Freight-In			5 4 0 00	11
12			Wages Expense			23 2 0 0 00	12
13			Rent Expense			8 0 0 0 00	13
14			Supplies Expense			9 0 0 00	14
15			Telephone Expense			2 6 0 0 00	15
16			Utilities Expense			3 8 0 0 00	16
17			Insurance Expense			1 0 0 0 00	17
18			Depreciation Expense—Equipment			2 0 0 0 00	18
19			Miscellaneous Expense			3 0 0 00	19
20			Interest Expense			7 0 0 00	20
21							21
22		31	Income Summary		12 0 8 0 00		22
23			K. T. Morse, Capital			12 0 8 0 00	23
24							24
25		31	K. T. Morse, Capital		8 0 0 0 00		25
26			K. T. Morse, Drawing			8 0 0 0 00	26
27							27
28			Reversing Entry				28
29	20-2 Jan.	1	Wages Payable		2 8 0 00		29
30			Wages Expense			2 8 0 00	30

This page intentionally left blank.

PROBLEMS
Problem 5

Clark's Clothing
Work
For Year Ended

	ACCOUNT TITLE	TRIAL BALANCE DEBIT	TRIAL BALANCE CREDIT	ADJUSTMENTS DEBIT	ADJUSTMENTS CREDIT
1	Cash	16 4 0 0 00			
2	Accounts Receivable	7 1 0 0 00			
3	Merchandise Inventory	28 0 0 0 00		(b) 12 4 0 0 00	(a) 28 0 0 0 00
4	Supplies	3 0 0 0 00			(c) 9 0 0 00
5	Prepaid Insurance	2 0 0 0 00			(d) 5 0 0 00
6	Land	10 0 0 0 00			
7	Building	100 0 0 0 00			
8	Accum. Depr.—Building		10 0 0 0 00		(e) 10 0 0 0 00
9	Fixtures	33 0 0 0 00			
10	Accum. Depr.—Fixtures		6 0 0 0 00		(f) 2 0 0 0 00
11	Accounts Payable		9 0 0 0 00		
12	Wages Payable				(g) 3 8 0 00
13	Sales Tax Payable		1 2 0 0 00		
14	Unearned Revenue		10 0 0 0 00	(h) 7 0 0 0 00	
15	Mortgage Payable		58 0 0 0 00		
16	Alex Clark, Capital		73 3 0 0 00		
17	Alex Clark, Drawing	12 5 0 0 00			
18	Income Summary			(a) 28 0 0 0 00	(b) 12 4 0 0 00
19	Sales		225 5 0 0 00		(h) 7 0 0 0 00
20	Sales Returns and Allowances	2 0 0 0 00			
21	Sales Discounts	5 0 0 00			
22	Purchases	68 5 0 0 00			
23	Purchases Returns and Allowances		1 2 0 0 00		
24	Purchases Discounts		1 3 0 0 00		
25	Freight-In	4 4 0 00			
26	Wages Expense	19 8 0 0 00		(g) 3 8 0 00	
27	Advertising Expense	7 0 0 00			
28	Rent Expense	82 6 6 0 00			
29	Supplies Expense			(c) 9 0 0 00	
30	Telephone Expense	2 1 0 0 00			
31	Utilities Expense	1 8 0 0 00			
32	Insurance Expense			(d) 5 0 0 00	
33	Depr. Expense—Building			(e) 10 0 0 0 00	
34	Depr. Expense—Fixtures			(f) 2 0 0 0 00	
35	Miscellaneous Expense	6 0 0 00			
36	Interest Expense	4 4 0 00			
37		395 5 0 0 00	395 5 0 0 00	61 1 8 0 00	61 1 8 0 00
38	Net Income				
39					

Problem 5 (Concluded)

Store

Sheet

December 31, 20-1

ADJUSTED TRIAL BALANCE DEBIT	ADJUSTED TRIAL BALANCE CREDIT	INCOME STATEMENT DEBIT	INCOME STATEMENT CREDIT	BALANCE SHEET DEBIT	BALANCE SHEET CREDIT	
16 4 0 0 00				16 4 0 0 00		1
7 1 0 0 00				7 1 0 0 00		2
12 4 0 0 00				12 4 0 0 00		3
2 1 0 0 00				2 1 0 0 00		4
1 5 0 0 00				1 5 0 0 00		5
10 0 0 0 00				10 0 0 0 00		6
100 0 0 0 00				100 0 0 0 00		7
	20 0 0 0 00				20 0 0 0 00	8
33 0 0 0 00				33 0 0 0 00		9
	8 0 0 0 00				8 0 0 0 00	10
	9 0 0 0 00				9 0 0 0 00	11
	3 8 0 00				3 8 0 00	12
	1 2 0 0 00				1 2 0 0 00	13
	3 0 0 0 00				3 0 0 0 00	14
	58 0 0 0 00				58 0 0 0 00	15
	73 3 0 0 00				73 3 0 0 00	16
12 5 0 0 00				12 5 0 0 00		17
28 0 0 0 00	12 4 0 0 00	28 0 0 0 00	12 4 0 0 00			18
	232 5 0 0 00		232 5 0 0 00			19
2 0 0 0 00		2 0 0 0 00				20
5 0 0 00		5 0 0 00				21
68 5 0 0 00		68 5 0 0 00				22
	1 2 0 0 00		1 2 0 0 00			23
	1 3 0 0 00		1 3 0 0 00			24
4 4 0 00		4 4 0 00				25
20 1 8 0 00		20 1 8 0 00				26
7 0 0 00		7 0 0 00				27
82 6 6 0 00		82 6 6 0 00				28
9 0 0 00		9 0 0 00				29
2 1 0 0 00		2 1 0 0 00				30
1 8 0 0 00		1 8 0 0 00				31
5 0 0 00		5 0 0 00				32
10 0 0 0 00		10 0 0 0 00				33
2 0 0 0 00		2 0 0 0 00				34
6 0 0 00		6 0 0 00				35
4 4 0 0 00		4 4 0 0 00				36
420 2 8 0 00	420 2 8 0 00	225 2 8 0 00	247 4 0 0 00	195 0 0 0 00	172 8 8 0 00	37
		22 1 2 0 00			22 1 2 0 00	38
		247 4 0 0 00	247 4 0 0 00	195 0 0 0 00	195 0 0 0 00	39

Problem 6

1.

Clark's Clothing Store

Income Statement

For Year Ended December 31, 20-1

Revenue from sales:				
Sales			$232,500	
Less: Sales returns and allowances		$ 2,000		
Sales discounts		500	2,500	
Net sales				$230,000
Cost of goods sold:				
Merchandise inventory, Jan. 1, 20-1			$ 28,000	
Purchases		$68,500		
Less: Purchases returns and allow.	$1,200			
Purchases discounts	1,300	2,500		
Net purchases		$66,000		
Add freight-in		440		
Cost of goods purchased			66,440	
Goods available for sale			$ 94,440	
Less merchandise inv., Dec. 31, 20-1			12,400	
Cost of goods sold				82,040
Gross profit				$147,960
Operating expenses:				
Wages expense			$ 20,180	
Advertising expense			700	
Rent expense			82,660	
Supplies expense			900	
Telephone expense			2,100	
Utilities expense			1,800	
Insurance expense			500	
Depreciation expense—building			10,000	
Depreciation expense—fixtures			2,000	
Miscellaneous expense			600	
Total operating expenses				121,440
Income from operations				$ 26,520
Other expenses:				
Interest expense				4,400
Net income				$ 22,120

Problem 6 (Continued)

2.

Clark's Clothing Store		
Statement of Owner's Equity		
For Year Ended December 31, 20-1		
Alex Clark, capital, January 1, 20-1		$73,300
Net income for the year	$22,120	
Less withdrawals for the year	12,500	
Increase in capital		9,620
Alex Clark, capital, December 31, 20-1		$82,920

Problem 6 (Concluded)

3.

Clark's Clothing Store
Balance Sheet
December 31, 20-1

Assets			
Current assets:			
Cash		$16,400	
Accounts receivable		7,100	
Merchandise inventory		12,400	
Supplies		2,100	
Prepaid insurance		1,500	
Total current assets			$ 39,500
Property, plant, and equipment:			
Land		$10,000	
Building	$100,000		
Less accumulated depreciation	20,000	80,000	
Fixtures	$ 33,000		
Less accumulated depreciation	8,000	25,000	
Total property, plant, and equipment			115,000
Total assets			$154,500
Liabilities			
Current liabilities:			
Accounts payable	$ 9,000		
Wages payable	380		
Sales tax payable	1,200		
Unearned revenue	3,000		
Mortgage payable (current portion)	1,000		
Total current liabilities		$14,580	
Long-term liabilities:			
Mortgage payable	$ 58,000		
Less current portion	1,000	57,000	
Total liabilities			$ 71,580
Owner's Equity			
Alex Clark, capital			82,920
Total liabilities and owner's equity			$154,500

Problem 7

1.   Current Assets $39,500
    – Current Liabilities   –14,580
                               $24,920

2. $$\frac{\text{Current Assets}}{\text{Current Liabilities}} = \frac{\$39,500}{\$14,580} = 2.71 \text{ to } 1$$

3. $$\frac{\text{Quick Assets}}{\text{Current Liabilities}} = \frac{\$23,500}{\$14,580} = 1.61 \text{ to } 1$$

4. $$\frac{\text{Net Income}}{\text{Average Owner's Equity}} = \frac{\$22,120}{(\$73,300 + \$82,920)/2} = \frac{\$22,120}{\$78,110} = 28.3\%$$

5. $$\frac{\text{Net Credit Sales}}{\text{Average Accounts Receivable}} = \frac{\$115,000}{(\$8,400 + \$7,100)/2} = \frac{\$115,000}{\$7,750} = 14.84$$

    $365 \div 14.84 = 24.6$ days

6. $$\frac{\text{Cost of Goods Sold}}{\text{Average Inventory}} = \frac{\$82,040}{(\$28,000 + \$12,400)/2} = \frac{\$82,040}{\$20,200} = 4.06$$

    $365 \div 4.06 = 89.9$ days

Problem 8

GENERAL JOURNAL   PAGE

	DATE		DESCRIPTION	POST. REF.	DEBIT	CREDIT	
1			Adjusting Entries				1
2	20-1 Dec.	31	Income Summary		28 0 0 0 00		2
3			Merchandise Inventory			28 0 0 0 00	3
4							4
5		31	Merchandise Inventory		12 4 0 0 00		5
6			Income Summary			12 4 0 0 00	6
7							7
8		31	Supplies Expense		9 0 0 00		8
9			Supplies			9 0 0 00	9
10							10
11		31	Insurance Expense		5 0 0 00		11
12			Prepaid Insurance			5 0 0 00	12
13							13
14		31	Depreciation Expense—Building		10 0 0 0 00		14
15			Accumulated Depreciation—Building			10 0 0 0 00	15
16							16
17		31	Depreciation Expense—Fixtures		2 0 0 0 00		17
18			Accumulated Depreciation—Fixtures			2 0 0 0 00	18
19							19
20		31	Wages Expense		3 8 0 00		20
21			Wages Payable			3 8 0 00	21
22							22
23		31	Unearned Revenue		7 0 0 0 00		23
24			Sales			7 0 0 0 00	24
25							25
26							26
27							27
28							28
29							29
30							30
31							31

Problem 8 (Concluded)

GENERAL JOURNAL

PAGE

	DATE		DESCRIPTION	POST. REF.	DEBIT	CREDIT	
1			Closing Entries				1
2	20-1 Dec.	31	Sales		232 500 00		2
3			Purchases Returns and Allowances		1 200 00		3
4			Purchases Discounts		1 300 00		4
5			Income Summary			235 000 00	5
6							6
7		31	Income Summary		197 280 00		7
8			Sales Returns and Allowances			2 000 00	8
			Sales Discounts			500 00	
9			Purchases			68 500 00	9
10			Freight-In			440 00	10
11			Wages Expense			20 180 00	11
12			Advertising Expense			700 00	12
13			Rent Expense			82 660 00	13
14			Supplies Expense			900 00	14
15			Telephone Expense			2 100 00	15
16			Utilities Expense			1 800 00	16
17			Insurance Expense			500 00	17
18			Depreciation Expense—Building			10 000 00	18
19			Depreciation Expense—Fixtures			2 000 00	19
20			Miscellaneous Expense			600 00	20
21			Interest Expense			440 00	21
22							22
23		31	Income Summary		22 120 00		23
24			Alex Clark, Capital			22 120 00	24
25							25
26		31	Alex Clark, Capital		12 500 00		26
27			Alex Clark, Drawing			12 500 00	27
28							28
29			Reversing Entry				29
30	20-2 Jan.	1	Wages Payable		380 00		30
31			Wages Expense			380 00	31